HARVARD THEOLOGICAL STUDIES
VIII

THE
DEFENSOR PACIS
OF MARSIGLIO OF PADUA

A CRITICAL STUDY

BY

EPHRAIM EMERTON
WINN PROFESSOR OF ECCLESIASTICAL HISTORY
IN HARVARD UNIVERSITY EMERITUS

30143

NEW YORK
PETER SMITH
1951

BIBLIOGRAPHICAL NOTE

THE most complete examination of the manuscripts of the *Defensor Pacis* thus far published is by an American scholar, Dr. James Sullivan, now State Historian of New York, " The Manuscripts and Date of Marsiglio of Padua's *Defensor Pacis*," in the *English Historical Review*, 1905, pp. 293–307. Dr. Sullivan personally examined twenty manuscripts in several European libraries and drew certain conclusions as to the date of composition of the *Defensor*. It is a matter of regret that other occupations have prevented him from carrying on his studies to the point of preparing a much needed new edition of the original. Meanwhile this work has been taken up by Professor Richard Scholz of Leipzig, and his edition, to appear in the *Monumenta Germaniae Historica* in a Section to be called *Tractatus de jure imperiali saec. XIII et XIV*, may be expected shortly.

A brief summary of the printed editions is given by Dr. Sullivan in an article on Marsiglio of Padua and William of Ockam in the *American Historical Review* for April and July, 1897. I have made use of the very imperfect edition of Goldast in his *Monarchiae Romani Imperii, etc.*, 3 vols. fol., Frankfurt, 1668, vol. II, pp. 154–312, and also of Professor Scholz's much abbreviated edition *in usum scholarum* in *Quellensammlung zur Deutschen Geschichte*, 1914.

No complete translation from the original has ever been made into any modern language, but partial translations have appeared in French (before 1363), Italian (1363, from the French), German (1545), and English. The English translation by William Marshall was published in 1535 and is now extremely rare. There are three copies in the Bodleian and one in the British Museum, but I am not aware of any copy in this country.

Up to the present time the most complete and satisfactory analysis of the contents of the *Defensor* is that given by Sigmund Riezler in his illuminating study, *Die literarischen Widersacher der Päpste zur Zeit Ludwig des Baiers*, 1874. All later writers have borrowed freely from this, but its conclusions have been modified on many points of detail. The most careful study of Marsiglio's life is that of Professor Baldassare Labanca of Padua, who writes from the point of view of a liberal Italian patriot with a strong tinge of local Paduan pride: *Marsiglio da Padova, Riformatore politico e religioso del secolo XIV*, 1882.

Shorter discussions of Marsiglio and related authors are to be found in: —

Friedberg, Emil, *Die mittelalterlichen Lehren über das Verhältniss von Staat und Kirche*, 1869. Zeitschrift für Kirchenrecht VIII, pp. 121–138.

Bezold, Friedr., *Die Lehre von der Volkssouveränetät während des Mittelalters*, 1876. Historische Zeitschrift XXXVI, pp. 343–347.

Müller, Carl, *Der Kampf Ludwigs des Baiern mit der Römischen Curia*, 1879–80.

Scaduto, Fr., *Stato e Chiesa negli scritti politici 1122–1347*. 1882.

Guggenheim, M., *Marsilius von Padua und die Staatslehre des Aristoteles*. Historische Vierteljahrschrift XV (7) 1904.

Dunning, W. A., A History of Political Theories Ancient and Mediaeval, 1905, pp. 238–244.

Stieglitz, L., *Die Staatstheorie des Marsilius von Padua*, 1914. Beiträge zur Kulturgeschichte des Mittelalters.

Lupold von Bebenburg: *de juribus regni et imperii Romani tractatus variarum rerum cognitione refertus. Basileae*, 1566.

Meyer, H., *Lupold von Bebenburg; Studien zu seinen Schriften*, 1909. Studien und Darstellungen aus dem Gebiete der Geschichte VII, 1–2.

Valois, Noël, *Jean de Jandun et Marsile de Padoue auteurs du Defensor Pacis*. Histoire Littéraire de la France XXXIII, pp. 528–623.

Baumann, J. J., *Die Staatslehre des heiligen Thomas von Aquino*, 1873.

Zeiller, J., *L'idée de l'état dans S. Thomas d'Aquin*, 1910.

Wicksteed, Philip H., Dante and Aquinas, 1913.

Cappa-Legora, A., *La politica di Dante e di Marsilio da Padova*, 1906.

THE DEFENSOR PACIS
OF
MARSIGLIO OF PADUA

I

To understand the importance of the political doctrines of Marsiglio of Padua one must bring them into relation with those of two of his not remote predecessors, Thomas Aquinas and Dante Alighieri. Aquinas died in 1274, three or four years after the birth of Marsiglio and Dante died in 1321, two or three years before the appearance of Marsiglio's great work, the *Defensor Pacis*. One might be tempted, therefore, to speak of these three notable contributors to political theory as representatives of contemporary thought. To do so, however, would be to miss the most essential quality in each. Aquinas, here as elsewhere in his monumental activity, is the spokesman of an epoch in human history that within a short generation after him was gone forever. Dante sounds the note of a transition just beginning to outline itself clearly in the rapid march of events. Marsiglio is the herald of a new world, the prophet of a new social order, acutely conscious of his modernness and not afraid to confess it. His book has often been called the most remarkable literary product of the Middle Ages, and I am inclined to accept this verdict. And yet, even the name of Marsiglio is unknown to most persons outside the narrow circle of students of political theory. Speaking to an audience of clergymen educated quite beyond the ordinary level of their class, I found that there was but one in the company who had ever heard Marsiglio's name, and that was only because he had been a pupil of mine in his university days.

The explanation of this obscurity is, I think, not far to seek. The teaching of Marsiglio entered so subtly but so completely into the doctrine of his successors in the work of national development and of church reform that it has been overshadowed by their greater fame. From Wycliffe to Luther his influence can be traced with entire distinctness. It is seen sometimes, though rarely, in open acknowledgement of indebtedness, oftener in unmistakable similarities of argument, and again in the unsparing criticism of orthodox opponents. His name is the most hated in the whole category of critics of the mediaeval order, and justly, for the defenders of the existing system perceived from the first that Marsiglio, more accurately than any one before him, had put his finger on the sore spot of European civilization as worked out on the mediaeval theory of society. The limit of that theory, as developed by Thomas Aquinas in all his voluminous writing, had been reached. Sooner or later it must give way before a new spirit of criticism and a new sense of power in social elements that had hitherto been denied their right of expression. How soon that was to be no man in the early fourteenth century could foresee, but the travail of the new time was beginning, and Marsiglio's teaching was its potent agent.

The world of Thomas Aquinas was dominated by a few great simple universal ideas, of which the life of man, both individual and associated, was the reflex. At the heart of things was God, revealed in the uniformity and harmony of Nature. The center and crown of creation was Man, to whom was given the rule over the earth, which again was the center of the material universe, served by the obedient sun and accompanied by the planetary and the starry host in tributary homage. Corresponding to this majestic order of Nature, the associated life of man was also an image of ordered unity. It had, to be sure, its varieties of race and nation and social class, but these varieties were only the differentiations of an essentially unified existence. The one and only God had made one sole and sufficient revelation of himself, and this revelation had included a scheme of social order. Divine Providence had chosen for the moment of its revelation a point of time when the world was all united under the one beneficent, peaceful sway of the Roman Empire, and had demonstrated its purpose by bringing into one efficient and harmonious whole the two dominant forces of this Empire and the Christian Church, the supreme trustees of its revelation.

All history since the beginning of Christianity had been the further demonstration of this divine purpose. The unity of the Church, through the continuing power of the divine will, had been embodied in the institution of the Roman Papacy, the one single depositary of the leadership of Christ through his one chosen agent, Peter, the leader of the Apostles. The unity of civil society had been secured by the continuation of the Roman imperial power, transferred in due time from the rebellious East to the subservient West in the persons of successive rulers, whose imperial claim the kings of the earth had acknowledged with willing submission. And these two unities of Church and of State, were in essence but one; for, as the spiritual is higher than the material, as the sun is brighter than the moon, so was the spiritual power in the last resort superior to the temporal. Each was but an illustration within its own peculiar sphere of that divine sovereignty under which by the very definition of God all lesser rule belongs.

It mattered not at all to the defenders of this magnificent theory that in fact a great majority of Christians refused to submit to the headship it implied. It was of no account that no trace of such a headship could be found until ten generations of Christians had passed their lives under a totally different conception of church order. It was convenient to forget that as between the two branches of the divine administration of western Christendom there had never existed that harmony which the whole theory of papal headship assumed. All these apparent limitations were only the accidents proper to all institutions entrusted to human hands. The theory persisted, and the thirteenth century — "greatest of Christian centuries" in the calm judgment of its admirers — had seemed to put the seal upon its triumph. From Innocent III to Boniface VIII the Papacy had been able to celebrate a series of victories over its secular opponents, the national governments, the national episcopates, and the spokesman for all these temporal interests, the mediaeval Empire.

It is this triumph of the mediaeval theory of society that forms the background of the extraordinary activities of Thomas Aquinas. By whatever other name he may be known, the

most significant word to describe him is the one he himself
suggests, the "Summarist." Not only in his greatest work,
the "*Summa Theologiae*," but throughout his enormous literary
product, he gives us as in a mirror the reflection of the fixed
conditions of thought by which the society of his day was
governed. Contemporaries of his in the field of public and
private law were putting forth books of law which they called
"mirrors" (*Spiegel*). So Thomas mirrored to his generation
and to all succeeding generations, the philosophic, the religious,
the social, and the political ideals of his time. To him as to
the men of the thirteenth century in general, these ideals
seemed to express not so much aims of the future as actually
accomplished facts. The ideal seemed to have taken shape in
institutions that must endure forever.

In his treatment of the state as the most important form of
human association Thomas follows almost completely the lead
of Aristotle. He approves the monarchy as the best type of
government, because it offers the best security against disorder.
He draws, however, a sharp line between the monarch and the
tyrant. To prevent the single ruler from degenerating into
tyranny he would have him limited by some constitutional
restraint on the part of the best elements of the population,
but he is, perhaps purposely, vague as to the precise nature of
this restraint. His monarch must be a "good" man, that is
he must have for his guiding principle the welfare of his subjects. It is interesting to note that he nowhere discusses the
nature of the Empire as distinguished from other forms of
monarchical government. He assumes that there will be
many different groupings of men around many leaders, and
what he says as to the duties and obligations of the ruler
applies to all alike. He makes no criticism of the imperial
idea as such, and he doubtless assumes the existence of such a
coördinating power among the principalities of Christendom.
Why then should he not have given to this quite unique element in the Christian commonwealth a treatment proportioned
to its historic as well as to its theoretical importance?

The answer to this problem may, perhaps, be found in
Thomas's supreme interest in the Church as the one coördinating force needed to give balance and harmony to the politi-

cal structure of the Christian state. To have elaborated after his fashion the rôle of the Empire as the arbiter and guarantor of peace among the states might well have seemed to him to be raising its function as at once the colleague and the rival of the Papacy to the danger point. Aquinas was not likely to forget in any theoretical idealism the practical facts of his present-day politics. During the whole period of his literary activity the twin powers of the mediaeval scheme had been fighting out their eternal conflict to what may well have seemed to him a final finish. In 1250 Frederic II, the embodiment of all that was most hateful to the papal interests, died defeated and discredited. His vast plans for the union of Germany with southern Italy had been scattered by the death of his son Manfred on the field of battle and of his grandson Corradino on the scaffold. All this had been accomplished by the unwearied diplomacy of the papal administration. So that, when Aquinas died in 1274 there was good reason to suppose that imperialism had done its work and was ready to give up the struggle. The election of Rudolf of Habsburg in the previous year had seemed to set the seal upon this conclusion; for his election was won at the price of a clear understanding that henceforth the things of Caesar were no longer to be confounded with the things of God.

That gives us the key note of Aquinas's thought on the whole subject. The cause of the long conflict between the temporal and the spiritual as embodied in the Empire and the Papacy, had been the confusion of their respective powers. The Empire was partly a divine institution; the Papacy, whatever disclaimers it might put forth, was at least equally a political institution. In the scheme of Aquinas this confusion disappears. Aside from and above all human law there must be a divine law. The purpose of human laws is to promote the earthly welfare of civil society. The object of the divine law is to direct men, both individually and socially, toward their highest end, the attainment of everlasting life. The administration of this divine law is in the hands of the Church, and the unity necessary for its efficiency is secured by the headship of the successor of Peter.

This unity is necessary in all matters in which the Church

as a whole is interested, especially in the uniformity of doctrine, without which there could be no real unity of structure. In case of doubt as to doctrine it is the pope alone who has the right to declare the truth. Here, almost precisely six hundred years before its formal declaration as an article of faith, we have the principle of papal infallibility definitely enunciated. No wonder that Aquinas has been proclaimed by the modern Papacy as the chief champion of the Roman tradition. But this is not the whole of it. While Aquinas tries to limit the power of Rome strictly to the declaration of the faith, he does not hesitate to draw the inevitable conclusion. The power which defines the faith in general is obviously the power which also determines in a given case whether an individual has departed from the faith. If then a ruler over Christian people is convicted by this last tribunal of having departed from the faith, what is the effect upon his relation to his people?

The argument here is very close. The Church does not punish him for his defect of faith; it only defines it. Its discipline extends only to separation from the body of the faithful. But the ruler so separated is placed outside the order of righteousness upon which rests the obligation of his subjects to obedience. As soon, therefore, as his excommunication is pronounced the subjects are *ipso facto* released from their allegiance. It is unnecessary to enlarge upon the enormous range of this simple declaration. It places within the power of one fallible man, however supported by the judgment or the interests of other fallible men, first to define a crime, then to apply this definition in a specific case, and then to overturn the order of a civil community by the simple declaration of his decision. It is based upon the ghastly proposition that independent judgment in regard to fundamental questions of religion is a crime fatal to the order of the civil community and therefore to be repressed by the civil power. The crime of heresy consists in the exercise of such independent judgment in regard to religion, and its definition could be — and was — indefinitely extended to cover any form of offence against the dominant power of the Church expressed through its agent, the Vicar of Christ at Rome. The ruler who set himself in opposition to the Papacy incurred the imminent risk of being declared a heretic and thus of losing his hold upon the allegiance of his subjects.

The political doctrines of Aquinas work out, therefore, to the ultimate supremacy of the papal government over all the civil authorities of Christendom. If they could ever be realised the result would be a monstrous theocracy within which every independent activity, whether of the individual or of organized society must shrivel and perish. That they had not been realized up to the time of Aquinas had been largely due to the unflagging energy of those representatives of the imperial power, men like Otto the Great, Henry IV, Frederic Barbarossa, and Frederic II, who had made themselves the champions of all national interests in their long struggle for recognition. The abandonment of this championship by Rudolf of Habsburg threw the responsibility for maintaining the rights of civil government upon the several national kingdoms.

In this new phase of the conflict the leadership passes from Germany to France. The final, or what appeared to the men of Aquinas' generation to be the final, triumph of the papal over the imperial policy had been brought about largely through the introduction of French influence into Italy to counteract the pressure of Germany. Within less than a generation after the death of Aquinas it became clear that in thus calling upon France to serve its cause in Italy the Papacy had summoned a servant likely at any moment to turn into a master, a master so much the more dangerous as it was free from all the tradi tions of theoretical loyalty that had at times restrained the action of the Empire. Back of every effort on the part of the French government lay the steadily increasing sense of French nationality and a constantly growing willingness to make sacrifices for it.

By the close of that first generation after Aquinas the papal chair was occupied by a Frenchman and had been removed from Rome to Avignon, there to remain continuously occupied by Frenchmen and subject to the immediate pressure of French political necessity during two generations to come. The process

tried to put these into literary form, both found in Aristotle formulas ready to their hand which could be interpreted in such ways as would serve their turn. "Originality," as we use the word, was not a mediaeval virtue. To have put forth ideas as one's own would in that day have been to invite disaster. The only way to gain a hearing was to pile up authorities; the only precaution needed was to make sure that one's authorities were sound.

It was, we may be sure, not pride of scholarship, or at least not this alone, that led men of the intellectual quality of Aquinas and Dante to fill their pages so largely with Aristotelian reference and method of demonstration. It was that they desired to give to what were really their own opinions the required sanction of acknowledged authority. It was in every respect parallel to their use of Scripture for the same purpose. Probably, in the case of Dante, the same may be said of his use of "science." The obscure and bewildering applications of mathematical and astronomical processes to the movement of human affairs had doubtless its effect in commending the value of the ideas thus hopelessly muddled up with irrelevant or misleading conceptions.

Dante shares with Aquinas the general notion of the State as a necessary organism designed primarily to maintain among men that condition of ordered peace without which the legitimate objects of human desire cannot be secured. He too thinks of human society as the reflex of a divine order. He sees the need of a divine representation on earth to secure the consecration of this society to the highest ends of man's existence both in this world and in the life to come. He parts company with Aquinas at the point of considering the means by which this highest control shall be administered. Thomas, as we have seen, has a very lofty conception of the function of the state, but in the last analysis the earthly ruler is subject to the constant revision of his acts by the superior power of the Church, and this right of supervision is centered in the one supreme jurisdiction of the Roman primate. Dante, on the other hand, believed that the primacy of Rome was only one part of the divine representation in the government of the

Christian commonwealth. Co-ordinate with it goes, in his doctrine of sovereignty, the function of the Empire, and this, not in virtue of any right conferred upon it by any earthly sanction, but independently, by its very nature.

This doctrine of imperial supremacy is set forth in a separate pamphlet with an argumentative defence probably convincing, at least to the Ghibelline intelligence of Dante's day, and having the merit, rather rare in a mediaeval document, of entire clearness in its main position. The treatise *De Monarchia* deals, not as is often supposed, with the question of monarchical government as compared with other forms of administering political states, but with the problem of a single administration for all states together. In other words it is a glorification of the idea underlying the Empire of the Middle Ages as the continuation of the imperial system of ancient Rome. The date of its composition is uncertain, but it is altogether probable that it is to be set somewhere near the year 1310, the date of the brilliant attempt of the Luxemburg emperor, Henry VII, to revive the glorious days of the Hohenstaufen and to wipe out the disgrace, if such it were, of the Habsburg compromise of a generation previous. As to Dante's feeling about the importance of such an imperial revival there can be no doubt whatever. He had appealed to the Habsburger Albert with all the fervor of a poet and a patriot to come down and rescue Italy from the chaos of party strife. He had written to the Italian cardinals to use all their influence to bring back the Papacy to its rightful place and its bounden duty toward the common fatherland. It is quite possible that he was one of the band of Italians who went to meet their "Savior" as he descended from the Alps and began his first triumphal progress through the Lombard plain.

The *De Monarchia* in its three books develops in logical order and according to the scholastic syllogistic method the principle of a single universal sovereignty for the world. The rule of one is better than the rule of many because it conforms to the law of Nature and because it is best suited to the ends for which human society exists. These ends are mainly peace and justice. Peace is possible only under the control of a

supreme prince.   This does not mean that all other lordships
are to be abolished.   Diversities of rule are a necessity; but,
since they are bound to produce diversities of desire, they must
be regulated by some superior tribunal.   But justice among
conflicting elements is possible only to a power which has no
interest in the questions at issue.   The emperor is such a power,
because being the supreme ruler he has nothing to gain.   He
represents in the things of this world the loftiest principle of
Christian charity, whereby he is able to maintain peace and to
distribute justice.   So far Dante's argument for single rule
follows that of Thomas and in general that of Aristotle.   He
concludes this first part with a characteristically naïf Christian
turn: — Christ chose for the time of his appearing on earth
the first moment since Adam when the whole world acknowledged the sovereignty of one imperial power.

But this monarchy belongs by right to Rome, and the second
book goes on to demonstrate this proposition.   Here Dante is
deserted by his Aristotle and becomes dependent upon his
own ingenuity.   Rome has a right to supreme rule because the
Romans were the noblest of peoples, as shown by the genealogy
of Aeneas, who derived his origin from all the noblest sources
of the ancient world.   Rome gained her power by miraculous
means, proving the special care of God for her preservation
and expansion.   Her wars were undertaken for the good of the
peoples;   her ends were therefore right, and, the ends being
right, it follows that the means she employed were right also.
The Romans were created fit to rule, hence were fulfilling their
destiny and therefore were right.   Supremacy acquired by
single combat is justly acquired, because in single combat
there is no enmity between the combatants, but only a desire
to seek the judgment of God.   Now Rome did thus acquire
power, and therefore had a right to it.   Finally again, Christ
by being born and accepting death under the rule of Rome
proved her right to rule.

Whatever one may think of the value of this logic, the point
is clear enough, and the third book clinches the "argument."
Its thesis is that the imperial power is independent of all
human control.   From God alone it derives its right to regu-

late the affairs of Christendom. The Empire existed before
the Church. The Donation of Constantine to the See of
Peter, which Dante of course in common with the mediaeval
world in general believed to be a genuine document, rested
upon this imperial right, otherwise Constantine would have
been granting what he had no power to bestow. The alleged
transfer of power by the Church from the eastern to the western ruler in the person of Charles the Great was impossible
because there was no possible source from which such right
of transfer could have been derived. Hence the necessity of
a two-fold leadership of the Christian commonwealth, a spiritual and a temporal. . . . The imperial Electors were not
electors in the strict sense, but rather heralds whose function
it was to proclaim the decision of divine Providence.

While thus repudiating in the most emphatic manner the
subjection of the Empire to the Papacy, Dante does not propose any remedy in case of conflict, but only presents his ideal
of the headship of the world. The emperor is bound to show
a filial regard for the person of the pope in order that he may
the more perfectly fulfil his own function of temporal leadership. It is here that we see the advance of Dante beyond the
ideals of Thomas Aquinas. His government of human society
is not a theocracy. Temporal and spiritual administration
are to be harmonized through the realization by the temporal
ruler of his divine origin and commission. The unfortunate
fact that this harmony, on which the whole structure of mediaeval society was theoretically based, had never in practice
been realized had nothing to do with the case. The failure
was due, not to the theory but to the frailty of human nature.
The remedy was now to go back to the pure standards of peace
and justice contained in Scripture and in the instruction of
the wise among the philosophers of the classic world.

III

The complete collapse of Henry the Seventh's Great Ad-
venture in Italy in the year 1313 was the demonstration, if
one had been needed, of the futility of Dante's dream of im-

perial restoration on the mediaeval basis. It leads us naturally to a brief survey of the political background of Marsiglio
of Padua. The death of Henry was followed by a divided
election in Germany A Habsburg candidate, Frederic of
Austria, and an anti-Habsburg candidate, Ludwig of Bavaria,
divided the electoral vote between them. Neither would give
way, and the decision was left to the ancient arbitrament of
war. A struggle of eight years ended in 1322 in the defeat of
Frederic and the acknowledgment of Ludwig by the German
princes. Conflicts of this sort had always afforded to ambitious popes the most welcome opportunities for asserting their
claims as arbiters of the political fortunes of the Empire, and
Pope John XXII was not the man to let the chance escape him.
Frenchman as he was, and accepting in its full extent the accomplished fact of the papal residence in France, he threw
himself from the first with hearty support on the side of Austria.

The ancient weapons that had served in the days of Hilde-
brand and Innocent III and Frederic Barbarossa were fur-
bished up again for this new encounter. On the papal side
every effort was made to show that the imperial power was
valid only as it was confirmed by the papal sanction. The
imperial champions not only denied this and asserted the principle of imperial independence, but went far beyond it and
claimed in their turn rights of control over the papal office.
If this had been all, history might well have cried: "a plague o'
both your houses!" and let it go at that. But what lends an
entirely new interest to this new phase of the old conflict is the
volume of discussion it called forth and in this discussion the
new emphasis placed upon the fundamental questions as to
the essential nature of the two parties in opposition, the State
and the Church.

The Papacy of John XXII found itself confronted by a very
peculiar alliance. Opposition from the imperial interests was
to be expected, but a still more dangerous antagonist was developed in the house of its friends. It was just a hundred
years since the papal institution had taken on a new lease of
life through the support of a tremendous popular religious
enthusiasm expressing itself in the new Mendicant Orders and

especially in the Order of St. Francis. In the course of that century these orders had run through the usual stages of enthusiasm, of practical organization, and of adjustment to the standards of the world they had tried to reform. Naturally, however, this worldlifying of the Orders had called out a reaction toward the nobler aspirations of the founders, and this idealism had found expression in that wing of the Minorites known as the "Fraticelli," or "Spiritual Franciscans." Once again the old battle cry of "evangelical poverty" had been raised as the standard to which all grades of the clerical hierarchy ought to conform. Especially was this standard of unworldliness to be applied to the Papacy itself, and this at a moment when in its safe retreat at Avignon it was feeding a hungry horde of its own creatures on the proceeds of a novel and extremely promising system of taxation on benefices throughout the western world! Natural enough, that a John XXII should reply to such an audacious suggestion by a decree of heresy against the Fraticelli, and that they should retort by a like charge against him. Not that this bandying back and forth of heresy charges was in itself of any great importance. It was useful only as calling out the defences on either side, in which the real issues of the combat are revealed.

Between these two enemies of the Avignon Papacy, the Empire and the "radicals," if one may so call them, of the Franciscan order, there was thus prepared the basis of an alliance that was to be of decisive importance in the immediate future. Each turned to the other for the kind of support which it specially needed and which the other was specially capable of giving. Ludwig, in his fight for supremacy over the papal power, needed every possible weapon on the legal and philosophical side of his contention. The Fraticelli, strong only on this ideal side, needed every possible security against actual physical persecution by the papal arm. Whatever could be done to show the extravagant worldliness of the Papacy in the strongest light was in so far a contribution toward the general clearing up of the mind of Europe on the whole broad question of the relation of the clerical to the civil powers.

It is through this peculiar alliance that the services of

Marsiglio of Padua were brought into play. It seems well established that he was not a member of the Franciscan or of any other religious order, but it is equally clear that in his studies and in his executive function at the university of Paris he had been brought into close relations with Franciscan activities. Especially indicated, though not positively proven, is his connection with the man who, more than any other, was coming to be the spokesman of that new philosophy of Nominalism which was destined to transform the thinking processes of Europe in transition, the English Franciscan, William Ockham. Precisely what were the relations between the two has been the subject of much study and speculation.[1] There is no doubt that, as the bearing of the nominalistic teaching upon the papal claims became more apparent, the work of Marsiglio came to be thought of as the natural product of so perverted a condition of the intellectual process. He must, it was felt, have been a pupil of Ockham; from no other source could such pestilent doctrines have been derived. In the condemnations of his work dating from 1327 on he is often expressly described as a follower of Ockham's teaching. On the other hand there is but slight evidence of actual collaboration between the two, and perhaps the safest conclusion is that each influenced the other in the way best suited to his peculiar genius and talent. Ockham was primarily a philosopher interested, as a philosopher is bound to be, in discovering general principles of thought applicable to all intellectual problems. Marsiglio was primarily a political theorist employed in defending the rights of civil authority against what he represented as encroachments upon these rights by a power outside the range of civil control. In this defence the principle of the new philosophy was a most valuable ally, and he followed it, not avowedly as a disciple, but practically, as one whose own mental process was naturally akin to that of the acknowledged leader of the school.

Precisely how the emperor Ludwig came to know these two champions of causes closely allied to his own is obscure but may

[1] Sullivan, James; *Marsiglio of Padua and William of Ockam.* American Historical Review, April and July, 1897.

easily be guessed. Ockham had identified himself early with the "spiritual" wing of the Franciscans. He was a notable member of the order, later becoming its General. It could hardly fail that in the appeals of the order to the protection of the Empire, his name should have been prominent as the most vigorous exponent of its cause. The case of Marsiglio is a little more difficult. Up to the time of his entrance into the great conflict he had been known only as a scholar and university man, not identified with "causes" and not associated with ruling powers anywhere. It is altogether possible that, having something to sell, he took his wares to the market where they would best be appreciated. It is to the credit of the hard pressed Ludwig that he recognised promptly the value of the contribution thus offered to him and became the patron under whom Marsiglio was to serve during the brief period of his public activity. The anecdote told of Ockham's first personal dealings with the emperor applies equally well to Marsiglio: "If you will protect me with your sword" the philosopher is reported to have said, "I will defend you with my pen."

Many attempts have been made to show that the *Defensor Pacis* was the joint product of Marsiglio and a French colleague of his at the university of Paris, John of Jandun. The most recent of these is by M. Noël Valois in the *Histoire littéraire de la France*, t. xxxiii, pp. 528–623 (1906). His article is entitled: *Jean de Jandun et Marsile de Padoue auteurs du Defensor Pacis*. The author gives a detailed account of the philosophical treatises which form the bulk of Jandun's literary product. These are all of a highly speculative, metaphysical character and are not concerned with political or ecclesiastical problems. Their tendency is to a mild scepticism on the vexed question of the "reality" of general concepts. Indeed it is not on any marked similarity of views that M. Valois bases his opinion as to the collaboration of Jandun with Marsiglio.

This, he declares is a *"fait avéré."* Contemporaries, "who doubtless knew better than we what the truth of the matter was," always couple the two together. Of this he gives four examples:

1. A contemporary Latin "poem," *De Bavari apostasia,*

edited by O. Cartellieri in *Neues Archiv der Gesellschaft für ältere deutsche Geschichtskunde*, Bd. xxv, pp. 712–715 (1899). The author does indeed join the names of Jandun and Marsiglio in a common indictment as *serpentini gemini.* He says that they wrote *codicillos, cartulas, et libellos,* and that they made false commentaries upon texts they did not understand. He had heard them both lecture upon *naturalia,* but even then their imagination had opened the way to contention (*discrimen*). There is no mention of the *Defensor Pacis* and no reference to collaboration in this or any other work.

2. The French continuator of the Chronicle of Guillaume de Nangis (ed. Géraud, ii, p. 74) describes the reception of Marsiglio and Jandun at the court of Ludwig, but he also makes no reference to the *Defensor Pacis* or to collaboration in any one book. He quotes as theirs certain opinions hostile to the papal supremacy and says that Ludwig protected them reluctantly without endorsing their views.

3. The judicial examination at Paris of a certain Francesco of Venice, an alleged *famulus* of Marsiglio, given in Baluze, *Miscellanea*, ii, p. 280 (1761). The young man says that Marsiglio and Jandun, and they alone, composed "a certain book," which, so far as he knew, contained no errors such as were charged upon them. If it had, he would not have failed to report them to the bishop of Paris. The obvious purpose of this deposition was to clear the youth himself and everyone else except the two persons directly charged. In any case it is extremely slight evidence as to actual collaboration.

4. The bulls of John XXII directed against the emperor Ludwig and against Marsiglio and Jandun make repeated reference to "a certain book" which they presented to the emperor and which furnished him support in his conflict with the papal power. There can be no reasonable doubt that the book thus referred to was the *Defensor Pacis*, or that the papal writer believed it was the expression of opinions held jointly by the two Parisian masters. As proof of joint composition such an estimate cannot go very far.

That is the most that can be said for a participation of John of Jandun in the writing of the *Defensor Pacis*. On the other side is the internal evidence, borne by every line, of unity in plan, in purpose, and in style.   If any one worked with Marsiglio it must have been in a very subordinate capacity.   A man of Jandun's undoubted quality could hardly have taken an important part in the work without leaving far more distinct traces of his activity than M. Valois has been able to show. In his brief analysis of the *Defensor* he simply assumes the double authorship without attempting to discriminate in any way between the contributions of the two alleged authors.

IV

The facts of Marsiglio's life are meagre and uncertain.   He was born in Padua probably about the year 1270, of good, but not specially notable family.   He left Padua as a young man and migrated to Paris, the natural goal of all intellectually ambitious youths of his day.   He may have broken his journey by a visit to Orleans, and may there have studied the elements of the Roman Law, though only slight traces of a knowledge of that law are visible in his writings.   At Paris he was certainly the Rector of the famous University in the year 1312, but our only information of his activity is in one or two documents bearing his name.   He left Paris, perhaps in the year 1324, and reached Nuremberg in 1326.   He was there received with enthusiasm by the emperor, Ludwig the Bavarian, in whose service he remains as long as we are able to trace his career at all.   In the following year he went with Ludwig to Italy as his most trusted counsellor.   He stood by the emperor through the exciting experiences of the ensuing months, supplying him with ammunition in his combat with the absentee Papacy at Avignon and witnessing the outward triumph of the ideas which he had embodied in the great treatise we shall soon have to examine.   He shared with Ludwig the inevitable overturn in Roman-papal politics and set out with him on his return to Germany in 1328.   There he disappears from our sight.   The Florentine historian Giovanni Villani states casually (Book x, c. 100) that he died in Italy just a month after leaving Rome.[1]   Much later local historians of Padua report that he was reconciled to the politic pope John XXII and made Archbishop of Milan.   There is some reason to believe that the emperor, in his negotiations with the pope eight years later, promised to discipline Marsiglio; but that is all.

This man, whose influence was felt throughout the whole period of two hundred years between the appearance of the *Defensor Pacis* and the advent of Martin Luther, vanishes from contemporary notice as completely as if he had never put pen to paper.   His identity as a man is lost in the one great work by which he has lived.   The *Defensor Pacis* interests the modern student in virtue both of its contents and its methods. What distinguishes it from its immediate predecessors and also from much of the product of the century and more following is its note of modernity.   It is the obvious expression of opinion of an individual, fortified it is true, by abundant if not superabundant reference to authorities, but at every point revealing independence of all authority.   Frankly the work of an advocate, expressly intended to support the cause of one of the great parties in a world struggle, it seeks to bring this advocacy of a party into relation with great general principles. Marsiglio has no hesitation in using the first person.   "I will now prove," "I think," "I have demonstrated," are frequent phrases.   Everywhere one feels the personality of a thinking man.

The first clear impression derived from the continuous reading of the *Defensor Pacis* is that it is all of one piece.   It begins with definitions, moves on to the application of these definitions to specific instances, and concludes by bringing these specific cases again into their proper subordination to definition.   Continually there is reference both backward and forward, showing that before the work left the author's hands it was thoroughly reviewed and cast into one completed whole.   Its Latinity would make the ghost of Cicero weep,

---

[1] M. Noël Valois, in the article referred to above, makes the ingenious suggestion that the person whose death is reported by Villani is not Marsiglio, but John of Jandun, who disappears at this time and to whom the abusive epithets of the Florentine chronicler apply equally well.

but it has the primary merit of expressing quite precisely the author's thought. There are very few passages the meaning of which does not become clear when one reads them in the light of all the rest. The badness of the Latin comes from its nearness to the thinking process of the writer, in other words from his modernness, and this only brings him so much the nearer to our own ways of putting things. Such Latin as this any one of us might write if he were well grounded in vocabulary and proportionally indifferent to syntax.

Especially notable is his departure from the favorite mediaeval syllogistic method. Occasionally he drops into it with a casual reference to a major or a minor premise, but in general his reliance is not upon the formal soundness of logical propositions, but upon the inherent truth or the self-evident common sense of his ideas. His process is fore-shadowed by the division of his work into three "*dictiones*," i. e. statements. He does not offer subjects for argument; he makes statements, and then proceeds to demonstrate them by explanation and elaboration. He is anxious, not so much to prove his point by contentious discussion as to present it in a variety of lights and then leave it to the fair judgment of the reader's good sense and right intention. It is this method which has brought upon Marsiglio the reproach of vain repetition, and it is true that he does repeat a good deal. A reader concerned only with the main argument would find this annoying, but examined carefully it does not appear quite vain. Each repetition occurs in connection with some new way of presenting the given thought, and the long result is not to confuse but to clarify.

It would be of interest to know whether the *Defensor Pacis* was written on the express commission of the emperor Ludwig the Bavarian or was the outcome of Marsiglio's independent thought and was then offered to the emperor as the patron most likely to find it of service and to reward it most handsomely. The fact that it is formally addressed to Ludwig gives no indication on this point; for if accepted by him it would certainly under any circumstances have been fitted with an appropriate dedication. On the other hand, in the dedica-

tion as it stands there is no hint of a commission, and I incline
to think that Marsiglio's profession is an honest one that he
is moved "to commit these opinions to writing" as a loyal
"son of the city of Antenor (Padua), by love of truth-telling,
by zealous devotion to his fatherland and his fellow-citizens,
by pity for the oppressed and a desire to save them and to
recall oppressors from the error of their ways, and to rouse
those who permit such things when they ought and can prevent
them, especially the emperor as the servant of God...after
long, close, and diligent examination, in the hope thereby to
be of assistance to you (the emperor) in your efforts to suppress
these evils and in other ways to serve the public good."

He proposes, with God's help, to set forth only the one
peculiar cause of the present conflict: "For to reiterate the
nature and number of those causes which Aristotle enumerates
would be superfluous; but from this cause, which Aristotle
could not know and which no one since his time has tried to
set forth, we hope so to lift the veil that it may henceforth
readily be banished from all civil communities, and when this
is accomplished that rulers and people of good will may live
in peace, the supreme desire of all men in this world and the
loftiest goal of human action." This one peculiar cause of
strife is the existence of the corrupt Church under the papal
administration.

Marsiglio has been further accused of inconsistency and
contradiction. I cannot find this charge substantiated by
facts. If his definitions are understood and accepted, his
statements hold together with a quite remarkable consistency.
From beginning to end there is no variation on essential points.
The third book, which he calls "Conclusions," sums up the
results of the first and second with continuous references to
specific passages binding the whole together. The most striking case of apparent contradiction, the defence of democracy
and at the same time the advocacy of the imperial rights, disappears when one follows carefully Marsiglio's analysis of the
imperial office as the representation of the ultimate right of
the people.

V

With these preliminary remarks we are prepared to follow the course of Marsiglio's thought as nearly as possible in the order in which it is presented in the work itself. The first book is devoted to a discussion of the principle of the State, the second to an examination of the origin and development of the Church, its appropriation by the Roman papal system, and its relation to the civil powers. The third is the brief summary of conclusions already mentioned. Marsiglio's first care is so to define his terms that there shall be no doubt in what sense he is using them. Like his predecessors he borrows the Aristotelian formulas as far as they suit his purpose. The State is a living organism, designed to secure to men those guarantees of order and the free development of capacity which shall lead to their highest good. Rulers there must be, but they are subordinate to the control of law. The definitions of law give us an excellent illustration of Marsiglio's analytical process. Law in its first meaning is a natural inclination toward a certain action or feeling, as for instance, when Paul says (Rom. 7, 23), "I see a different law in my members warring against the law of my mind." *Secondly,* law means a form or model in the mind for something to be made, as in Ezekiel (43, 12f.), "Behold, this is the law of the house; and these are the measures of the altar." *Thirdly,* law is a rule for such human actions as have reference to reward or punishment in the life to come. In this sense the Mosaic law is called "law" in some of its parts, and the Gospel law is so called in its entirety. In this sense also all "sects," as for instance that of Mahomet or the Persians, have "laws," though only the Mosaic and the Christian contain the truth. *Fourthly,* and more widely accepted, is the meaning of law as the whole body of opinion as to what is right and expedient in civil affairs and what is opposed to this opinion. Under this head may be distinguished a theoretical and a practical division, and the latter is to be taken as the definition of law in the strictest sense, because it implies behind the theoretical principle a *praeceptum coactivum*, a coercive sanction, which alone can give effect to the principle.

In this definition of law as a principle of right supported by the force necessary to put it into execution we have the key-note of Marsiglio's whole argument. It is only the power which has this coercive jurisdiction that can properly be entrusted with the application of law, and the whole thesis of the *Defensor Pacis* turns upon the distinction between the secular and the spiritual powers in this respect. His grievance is the invasion of the rights of secular authority by powers which are essentially spiritual and ought, therefore, to be restricted to the exercise of spiritual functions. The remedy is to be found in drawing as sharply as possible the lines of division between the two types of authority which have become obscured partly through the persistent aggression of the clerical and partly through the ignorance or indifference of the lay elements of the Christian society.

But now, whence comes this law which is to hold the balance amid the conflicting passions of a human community? In the answer to this question we find the most striking feature of Marsiglio's work. Without hesitation he declares that the source of law is to be found, not in any divine right of rulers, not in any superior wisdom of any class of society, but in the whole body of citizens.

"We declare that according to the Truth [1] and to the opinion of Aristotle, the Lawgiver, that is, the primary, essential and efficient source of law, is the People, that is the whole body of citizens or a majority of them, acting of their own free choice openly declared in a general assembly of the citizens and prescribing something to be done or not done in regard to civil affairs under penalty of temporal punishment. I say a majority, taking account of the whole number of persons in the community over which the law is to be exercised. [It makes no difference] whether the whole body of citizens or its majority acts of itself immediately or whether it entrusts the matter to one or more persons to act for it. Such person or

---

[1] I understand the word *veritas* to be used here and in many other passages as synonymous with Gospel.

persons are not and cannot be the Lawgiver in the strict sense, but only for a specific purpose and at a given time and on the authority of the primary lawgiver." Marsiglio seems to be guarding himself thus early in his inquiry against the charge afterward made against him that in emphasizing the rights of the people he was in so far minimizing the right of the emperor whose cause he was nevertheless defending. His point is that, within the scope of the powers given him by the people, the ruler cannot lawfully be interfered with by any other authority whatsoever.

The phrase here translated by the word "majority" (*pars valentior*) has been the subject of much discussion. Some writers have insisted that Marsiglio meant by it, not a numerical majority, but the more competent part of the body of citizens. I am convinced, however, by examining a great number of cases, that he was in truth a champion of the modern idea of majority rule as, on the whole, the best expression of the will of the whole community. In connection with the words *pars valentior* he frequently adds some further explanatory phrase which seems to indicate a numerical use, and the same idea is confirmed by the spirit of many of his references to the political sense of the lower orders of the people.

For example, speaking of the lawmaking process, he says: "The truth of a proposition is more accurately judged and its usefulness to the community more carefully taken into account when the whole body of citizens apply their intelligence and their feeling to it. For the greater number (*major pluralitas*) can detect a fault in a proposed law better than any part of them, as every corporate whole is greater in mass and in value (*mole atque virtute*) than any one of its separate parts." Marsiglio seldom mentions the *universitas civium* without adding, "or its *pars valentior*." Sometimes he uses *valentior multitudo* or *pluralitas*. He enlarges at great length on the importance of giving to all citizens some share in the government; he dwells upon the capacity of the humblest to do his part; but he nowhere describes any higher group as having special qualifications for citizenship. If by *pars valentior* he had meant "the more competent" or "the more highly placed" or "the more responsible," in other words any kind of an aristocracy, it is hardly conceivable that he should not have followed his invariable practice and given a precise definition of his meaning.

Speaking of the right to call a council (ii. 21) he says that this belongs to the Lawgiver, *i. e.* to the body of the faithful, because it or its *pars valentior* cannot so easily be seduced by selfish motives as can the Roman bishop or the College of Cardinals. Among the duties of the to-be-reformed pope is that of sitting as judge in strictly ecclesiastical cases with the *parte valentiori sive majori* of the college assigned to him by the Lawgiver. Here the meaning "majority" seems perfectly clear. Referring to the election of the emperor Marsiglio says that its validity depends upon the *valentiore parte* of those qualified to vote, a positive allusion to the principle of the majority as fixed in the Electoral College. In view of all these illustrations I feel no hesitation in regarding Marsiglio as a theoretical advocate of majority government.

What does Marsiglio mean by "citizens"? He answers this question with the Aristotelian definition: "I call a citizen one who has a share in the government of the civil community either in an executive or a judicial capacity, according to his degree." This excludes boys, slaves, foreigners and women, though in different ways; for boys are to become citizens in the near future. It is to the whole body of citizens thus defined that Marsiglio would commit the making of laws. The objection will be made that there are few wise and thoughtful persons, while the multitude of the simple (*stulti*) is infinite. But the greater part of the citizens are neither wicked nor lacking in judgment as regards the greater part of the questions that concern them and for the greater part of the time. (One is reminded of President Lincoln's immortal version of the same truth.) For all, or the greater part, are of sound mind and reason and of good will toward the state. Even though anybody and everybody does not originate laws, yet anyone is capable of a judgment in regard to matters originated by others and submitted to him, as to whether they ought to be added to or diminished or amended. The danger of legislation by a few is that they are likely to be moved by selfish interests rather than by the welfare of the community, "as has been abundantly shown in the decretal legislation of the clergy."

The process of lawmaking, therefore, should be as follows: Wise men, expert in the law, should be chosen in the general assembly of the citizens and entrusted with the framing of bills (*regulae*). "When these bills have been duly drawn up and carefully revised by these experts, they are to be submitted to the citizens in convention for amendment or rejection. Then, after everyone has been heard who has anything reasonable to say about them, again men are to be chosen or the former experts are to be confirmed, who as representatives of the authority of the body of citizens shall approve or reject the proposed bills in whole or in part; or this may be done, if they so choose, by the body of citizens themselves or the majority of them. After this approval, the so-called bills become 'laws' (*leges*) and are to be so designated, but not before. These alone, after being duly proclaimed, can bind those who violate them by civil penalties."

The ruler (*principans*) must govern according to the laws, but he must be of such quality that he can supplement them by what Marsiglio says he understands is called by jurists "equity," that is "the beneficent interpretation or moderation of the law in a specific case which is included in a rigid interpretation but might have been excepted if it could have been foreseen." To enforce the law the ruler should have a sufficient armed force, but this should not be allowed him until after his election. One feels here a reference to the repeated action of the German electors in choosing a not too powerful prince to be their *principans*. The ruler should have a large liberty of executive action, but should never be allowed to forget that whatever he does is done by him as the agent of the sovereign people. Marsiglio quotes with approval the Aristotelian maxim that all parts of the state should grow, like the parts of the human body, in due proportion, without the overgrowth of any one part, as, for example, of the multitude in a democracy, or, he adds, "of the priesthood under the Christian law."

Perhaps in consequence of his medical training, Marsiglio is especially fond of these analogies between the physical life and the life of the state. He never forgets that the state is a living organism with its directing force and its executive members. In the chapter on the origin of government (i. 15) he says:

"Like the action of nature in forming a perfect animal is that of the human mind in establishing a state and the parts thereof. . . . There is in nature a certain generative principle by which the body of the animal is formed and a certain distinctive quality (*virtutem*) given to each of its parts. The part first formed is the heart or a something comparable (*proportionalis*) to it. . . . This part first formed is nobler and more complete (*perfecta*) than the other parts of the animal. For generative nature has fixed in it a force and an instrumentality by which the other parts are formed out of appropriate material, are separated and distinguished one from the other, set in due relations, preserved in their characteristics, and protected against natural injuries. But if, through sickness or other check they fall away from the normal they are restored by the vigor (*virtus*) of this part.

"In the same way we should view the process of creating a properly constituted state. By the whole body of citizens as the soul (*anima*) there is or should be created a part comparable to the heart. In this is to be fixed a certain power or model (*forma*) with an active force or authority for establishing the other parts of the state. Now this part is the government (*principatus*), which in its causal aspect represents the universal law. Its active function is to administer justice, to issue commands, and to carry out just and expedient civil administration.

"This part in the state should be nobler and more perfect in its qualities, i. e. in prudence and virtue, than the other parts. . . . For the creative principle of the state, namely the community-soul, has fixed in this first part a certain universal causal force, which is the law, and also the executive power. Just as the natural warmth of the heart through which it performs all its activities is directed and regulated in its action by the structure and potency of the heart itself and could fulfil its purpose in no other way; furthermore, just as the heat called *spiritus* is regulated throughout the body by that same potency . . . so also the coercive power of government, entrusted to any man as an instrument, is analogous to the heat called *spiritus* and should be regulated by the law in dealing justice, in issuing orders, and in carrying out measures of civic expediency; for otherwise the ruler could not fulfil his purpose, which is the preservation of the state."

It might have been expected that Marsiglio, with his doctrine of the sovereignty of the people, would have been an advocate of a purely democratic form of government. Such, however, is not the case. He analyses the various kinds of rule, distinguishing carefully between democracy which he describes as the corruption of *politia*, that is a republic, in favor of the proletariat, the *egenorum multitudo*. Monarchy is the rule of one person for the good of all, in distinction from a tyranny, which is the rule of one for his own advantage. The monarchy he has in mind is a limited one (*temperatus principatus*), and rests upon the consent of the people, while a tyranny is independent of the popular will. Marsiglio does not declare himself abstractly in favor of any one type of government. He realizes that not all peoples, nor the same people at all times are fitted for the abstractly best of governments (*optimum principatuum*), and that therefore only the practically best under all the circumstances is to be expected; but it is this limited monarchy which is assumed in all his later treatment of the subject.

Whether this monarchy should be an hereditary or an elective one was obviously a matter of great importance in Marsiglio's scheme, and he gives to the discussion of this point a proportionally ample space. He first states the case of the opposition to election in twelve propositions and then proceeds to refute these one by one. The whole argument is summed up in the one principle, that inheritance gives similarity of body, but cannot be depended upon to give that continuity of spirit which is the greatest safeguard to the institutions of the state. The elected ruler is more likely to correspond to the "conformity of perfection" with his predecessors and with the principle of perfection in the whole universe of things than is the hereditary ruler.

This discussion leads naturally to the further inquiry whether there ought to be one single government for the whole civilized world (*civiliter viventium*). It is almost impossible not to connect Marsiglio's treatment of this question with the *De Monarchia* of Dante, which may have appeared within a dozen years before the *Defensor Pacis*. Marsiglio says that the subject is open to discussion, but is not pertinent to the present treatise. He does, however, go so far as to deny that the unity of the world is the model for the constitution of civil society. The Empire is a unit only in the sense that the several units of which it is composed submit themselves voluntarily to its supremacy, whereas the unity of the world depends upon some essential relation of each of its parts to a principle of unity at the center. The analogy, therefore, on which Dante bases his chief argument is expressly denied by Marsiglio. Nature, he thinks, seems to point rather toward multiplicity than towards unity, and he sees a possible purpose in this in order that, through wars and diseases of men and other animals, the population may be kept within the limits of sufficient support. Here is a touch of fourteenth century Malthusianism, but it is evident that Marsiglio feels himself here a little beyond his depth, and he turns the subject back to his own immediate field of discussion. Obviously too it would not do for him to go too far in diminishing the authority of the Empire he is defending.

The concluding chapter of the first book is a comprehensive statement of the purpose of the work as a whole. The object of government is to secure peace. Peace is the orderly working of all parts of the state according to the nature and purpose of each. It consists in the free interchange of the activities of the citizens, their mutual aid as against any hindrance from outside, and in the participation of all in the advantages of their common life, each in his own degree. The opposite of all this is discord. Thus much was known to Aristotle, but now comes in the Church as the disturbing element and with this the necessity of a new adjustment of powers. It is this cause which, by hindering the activities of its ruler, has deprived and still deprives "the Italian kingdom" of peace and its blessings and fills it with every sort of misery and injustice.

The immediate source of this evil of clerical supremacy Marsiglio finds in a change of theory as to the origin and development of the papal power. He rehearses briefly the establishment of a priestly order through the ordination of the Apostles, all of them equally, as the successors of Christ in the work of human redemption. That was enough down to the time of Constantine, but after that a claim "seems to have been derived from a certain grant which some say was made by Constantine to Sylvester. But then, either because this grant does not precisely formulate this claim or because it has lapsed through the progress of events, or was invalid as regards the other principalities of the world (or even as to the rule of the Romans in some of the provinces included in the grant) – for these reasons more recent bishops of Rome have based their coercive jurisdiction over the whole world upon another title, namely, upon the plenitude of power (*plenitudo potestatis*) which they claim was granted by Christ to St. Peter and his successors in the Roman See as Vicars of Christ.

In other words the Roman claim has been transferred from an historical basis to a theoretical one. The course of history brings changes; but a theory, if it can be maintained as a divine ordinance, does not change. In this was the obvious advantage of the Roman position and the most difficult point for its opponents to overcome. It is interesting to note that Marsiglio, more than a century before the complete exposure of the fraudulent Donation of Constantine by Lorenzo Valla casts a certain shade of doubt upon that universally accepted document. "Some say" that such a grant was made. Its contents are not specific as to Roman supremacy; its terms had become antiquated. One feels that if only the historic sense had awakened in the fourteenth as it did in the fifteenth century, the honor of that great exposure would surely have fallen to this fearless investigator.

"The title 'Vicar of Christ,' means, therefore, according to the Roman bishops, that, as Christ had plenitude of power and judgment over all kings, princes, communities, associations and individuals, so those who call themselves vicars of Christ and of St. Peter have plenitude of coercive jurisdiction not limited by any human law. . . . Popes are oppressing Italy on account of her divisions and her sufferings, but they overlook worse things in princes whom they fear. They gradually worm themselves (*serpunt*) into others' rights, especially those of the Empire during vacancies, until now they claim temporal coercive jurisdiction over all subjects of the Empire in Germany as well as in Italy."

This is the cause of the existing discord which prevents the emperor from exercising his power to keep the peace, and hence, all wise and powerful men should unite to check these usurpations. Marsiglio himself will use his learning to this end and is prepared to take the consequences.

VI

With the way thus prepared, Marsiglio enters upon the second and more important stage of his exposition. He antici-pates three kinds of opposition: first persecution by the Roman bishops and their "accomplices." They will oppose him because he is attacking their ambition for temporal riches and power. It will be idle to attempt to curb them by judicial argument: "May a merciful God restrain their fury and pro-tect the faithful, princes and people, whose peace is menaced by them." Here is the note of Luther's appeal to the German princes as the only possible defenders of the people's cause. The second kind of opposition will come from the false teach-ing of would-be leaders, the confusion of things temporal and things spiritual, the threatenings of eternal punishment to simple minded believers. Words simple in their original meanings have been perverted by gradual usage into false implications. So it will happen that many who read or hear these pages, especially those untrained in philosophy or in the Scriptures, will be checked at the outset. And then there will be the obstacle of malicious envy. Even men who know that what is here said is the truth will "rend it with the tooth of secret detraction or attack it with the noisy yelpings of presumptuous envy, simply because it is said by some one other than themselves." But Marsiglio will not be turned from his purpose by fear of any of these enemies.

Here again he begins with a series of very carefully guarded definitions, first of all with a definition of the Church. According to Aristotle *ecclesia* signifies the assembly of all the people belonging under one government. Among the Latins the word means, first and in the most popular sense, a building in which God is worshipped in common by the faithful, and then the officials, presbyters or (*seu*)[1] bishops, deacons and the rest who serve in such a building. In recent times (*apud modernos*) the Church means chiefly (*maxime*) those ministers, presbyters or (*seu*) bishops and deacons, who serve or preside in the metropolitan or chief of all churches, a position gained rather recently (*dudum*) by the church of the city of Rome, whose servants and presiding officers are the Roman pope and his cardinals. These now by a certain usage have gained the point, that they are called "the Church," and that the Church does or receives whatever they do or receive or ordain in any way whatsoever.

But in another sense, and this the most true and most appropriate of all according to the earliest usage and the intention of those who first employed it, the Church is the whole body of believers who call upon the name of Christ, and includes all parts of this body in whatever community they may be, even the community of the home (*etiam domestica*). Such was the primary use of the term among the apostles and in the primitive Church, and therefore all faithful followers of Christ, priests or not priests, are and of right ought to be called *viri ecclesiastici* "churchmen." To put it in other language: The Church consists of all those who belong to it, and here one sees the working in Marsiglio's mind of that philosophical

---

[1] Almost invariably when Marsiglio speaks of bishops and presbyters together he connects them by the word *seu*, hardly ever by *et* or *atque*. This seems to be one way of expressing his opinion on the essential equality of all ordained clergymen.

process of which his co-worker William Ockham was the most eminent spokesman. The unit of Christian fellowship was the individual Christian. It was not the order, the class, the official college, which determined the status of the individual; it was the body of individuals that gave sanction to every one of its organs. As the philosopher would have said: The *thing* was the reality, and the general concept was only a convenient name by which to express the complex of things — "*universalia post rem*," in distinction from the formula which had dominated the thought of the Middle Ages, "*universalia ante rem.*" It is this emphasis upon the right of the individual Christian man that runs like a scarlet thread throughout every stage of Marsiglio's further demonstration.

He goes on to distinguish between the words "temporal" and "spiritual." Temporal is readily defined as whatever pertains to the use and advantage of man in this world. The difficulty is in fixing the limits of the spiritual. Marsiglio enumerates no less than seven different senses in which the word is frequently employed. In general it may be used of all incorporeal things and their activities. More specifically it applies to the divine law, its teachings and its discipline, and so to the sacraments of the Church and their effects, the divine grace, all theological virtues and gifts of the Holy Spirit preparing us for the eternal life. Further, it may include all those voluntary human actions or experiences (*passiones*) which tend toward merit in the life to come, as, for example, divine contemplation, affection toward God and our neighbor, charities, fastings, prayers, pilgrimages, contempt of the world and escape from it. Less important is its application to the church building and all the apparatus connected with divine service.

But now, in the most recent times, certain persons extend this word "spiritual" most unsuitably and inappropriately to those actions of the clergy which are to the advantage or disadvantage of another person with reference to the present life. Still more improperly they include under "spiritual" the temporal possessions of the clergy, both real and personal, and also certain incomes from them which they call "tithes," so that under cover of this usage they may be exempted from the ordinary rules of the civil law. Surely this is an open abuse, and is contrary to the intention and practice of the apostles and saints, who called such things not "*spiritualia*," but "*carnalia seu temporalia*." "For not all their acts are spiritual or ought to be so called. Many of them are civil acts subject to contention, carnal, and temporal. For priests can borrow, make trusts, buy, sell, strike, kill, rob, fornicate, rape, betray, bear false witness, slander, fall into heresy, or commit other crimes, just as they are committed by laymen. Wherefore we may properly ask them whether any one of sound mind can call such actions when committed by them *spiritualia*."

The words *judex* and *judicium* offer another fine distinction. We use the word "judge" of an expert in some technical art, as, for example, of a physician, a geometer, or a carpenter, and his opinion within his field is a "judgment." Specifically, a judge is one having special knowledge of public or private law, commonly called an advocate, though in many regions, especially in Italy, he is called *judex*. Again, this word is used of the ruler, and his opinions are called *judicia* and have coercive power. Again and again in later chapters Marsiglio refers back to these fundamental distinctions in the use of terms in order to make perfectly clear in what sense he is using them at the moment and to guard himself against objections arising from their corruption or perversion. Especially in defining the powers of the priesthood he will insist upon the sharpest distinction between their character as experts and their claim to coercive jurisdiction.

The arguments for the coercive powers of the Papacy are summed up under the one principle that, as the spiritual is higher than the temporal, so that power which is primarily concerned with spiritual things has rights of control over all powers which have to do only with temporal things. Especially is this claim advanced as against the Empire, because the Papacy pretends to the right to confer the imperial power and to transfer it from one prince to another, as in the case of the famous transfer from the ruler of the east to the king of the Franks. This pretension has recently been renewed in the strongest terms in the conflict between Ludwig the Bavarian and his rival Frederic of Austria.   Marsiglio proposes to show "by the witness of Scripture in both its literal and its mystical sense, according to the interpretation of holy men and other approved doctors, that neither the Roman bishop called 'pope' nor any other bishop, presbyter, or deacon has a right to any sovereignty (*principatum*) or judicial authority (*judicium*) or coercive jurisdiction over any priest, ruler, community, association, or individual of whatsoever condition (understanding by 'coercive judgment' what we have already described as contained in the third meaning of *judex* and *judicium*)."

This sentence may be said to contain the thesis of the whole work.   It is a sweeping proposition, and Marsiglio seems to feel the necessity of safeguarding himself by a disclaimer. Here, he says, is no question as to what power or authority Christ, true God and true man, had and still has in this world, nor how much of such authority he had power to confer upon St. Peter, or upon the other apostles and their successors the bishops or presbyters; for on this point no true believer has any doubts.   What he wishes to investigate is the question, What executive power and authority in this world Christ *willed* to confer upon them and *de facto* did confer upon them, and from what he excluded and prohibited them both by his advice and his commands.   Christ came into the world, not to rule over men, not to judge them with judgments (according to the third meaning), not to be a temporal sovereign, but rather to subject himself to the conditions of the world as it was; nay, he purposely willed to exclude and did exclude himself and the apostles and disciples and consequently their successors, bishops or presbyters, from all temporal rule or sovereignty (that is, of a coercive character), and he did this by his example, his teaching, his counsel and his commands.

We are not greatly concerned with the long array of texts of Scripture and quotations from the Fathers from Augustine to Bernhard of Clairvaux.   This is notoriously a kind of argument that can be used with equal success on either side of any question.   The fact was, that the Church, in the narrower sense, had fortified itself with a tremendous structure of legal precedent and defiant assumption against which nothing short of determined revolt could accomplish any permanent result. The conclusion is the inevitable one, that since no clerical person has the right to coercive rule, all clergymen must be subject to the civil lawgiver, and may exercise jurisdiction over laymen or other clergymen only in so far as this is permitted to them by that lawgiver, in whose power, moreover, it lies to deprive them of it for reasonable cause. And it must not be forgotten that this "lawgiver" is, according to the definition, the People, acting either directly in assembly or through a ruler chosen by their own free action.

This leads naturally to an examination of the famous "power of the keys." Christ said to Peter (Matt. xvi, 19), "I will give unto thee the keys of the kingdom of heaven: and whatsoever thou shalt bind on earth shall be bound in heaven: and whatsoever thou shalt loose on earth shall be loosed in heaven." Similar sayings were addressed also to the whole body of the apostles (Matt. xviii, 18 and John xx, 23). What do they mean? Marsiglio answers in such a way as to show that he accepts the practice of the Church in committing to the priesthood the function of performing the sacraments and pronouncing the remission of sins upon due confession and repentance; but he shows also that the real process of absolution depends, not upon any action of the priest, but upon the grace of God freely given to the individual repentant soul. Confession is properly required, but if it is not practicable, then absolution takes place without it, provided, however, that the penitent have the honest intention of confessing at the first practicable opportunity. It is a modified protest, but the spirit of it is evident. The real thing is the individual will; the ceremony is accessory.

Marsiglio's authorities here are Peter Lombard and Richard of St. Victor, and he sums up his conclusion from their opinions: "From which it is evident that as regards the merit of the penitent, the Roman bishop has no more power than any other priest to absolve from guilt or from penalty. God alone absolves the truly penitent sinner without any action of the priest either preceding or accompanying." As to excommunication, although there is need of a priest to declare the decision, still the coercive function does not belong to any single priest or to any *collegium* of them.   It is the right of the whole body of the faithful in the community where the accused person belongs, or of his ruler (*superior*) or of a General Council to appoint a judge, whose duty it shall be to summon the accused, to examine him, to pass judgment, and to acquit him or condemn him to public disgrace and separation from the society of believers.   Nevertheless in the inquiry as to whether a person ought to be excommunicated or not, a judge of this sort should associate with himself a body of clergymen as experts in the law and the customary practice.   "If it were lawful for any one priest, either alone or with his *collegium* of clergymen, to excommunicate anyone he please without the consent of the whole body of the faithful, it follows that a priest or a *collegium* of them might take away all kingdoms and principalities from the kings or princes who hold them. For if any prince be excommunicated, all his subjects will be excommunicated also if they continue to obey him, so that the power of every prince will be destroyed."

By numerous analogies Marsiglio tries to make still clearer the distinction between the professional and the extra-professional action of the priesthood.   It is the function of the priest to examine the accused as to whether according to the Gospel law he ought to be cut off from the communion of the faithful lest he infect others; just as a physician or a council of them has to decide about a physical disease, e. g. whether a leper ought to be separated from human society.   But, as the physician has no coercive jurisdiction which would enable him to enforce such a decision, so the priest has no power to enforce his expert judgment.   In the same way, the turnkey (*claviger*) of a prison has the duty of opening and closing the doors, but has no power to say whether the door shall or shall not be opened to a given prisoner at a given time.   He has to proclaim that the prisoner is freed or not freed, but it is not his proclamation but the decree of the judge which really releases him. If he proclaim a man to be free or bound, contrary to the decree of the judge, the man is not therefore free or bound.   So the priest has the function of declaring the sinner absolved or condemned, but has no coercive right in the matter.

We now begin to see the practical applications of the distinctions thus carefully worked out. The first of these is the right of civil jurisdiction over the civil or temporal offences of clergymen. The fact already set forth that clergymen can and do commit crimes brings them of itself within the scope of the civil law; but Marsiglio goes a step further. The clergyman, as an expert in morals, sins more gravely and less excusably than the layman, and ought therefore to be the more severely punished. "Let no one object, that injuries by word of mouth or to property or to the person or of any other kind forbidden by secular law become "spiritual acts" when committed by a priest and that therefore their punishment does not belong to the secular ruler . . . for these are, as already shown, *carnalia* and *temporalia*. If the Roman bishop or any other priest were to be thus exempted from the coercive jurisdiction of rulers, and were himself to be a judge of this sort, freed from the authority of the human Lawgiver, and might separate all spiritual servants (commonly called "clergy") from the jurisdiction of rulers and subject them to himself (as the Roman pontiffs are doing in these days), it follows of necessity that the secular jurisdiction of rulers would be almost totally destroyed. That, I think, would be a serious evil and of great moment to all rulers and all communities."

In pursuance of their doctrine of clerical exemption, Roman bishops have recently been trying to include as many kinds of persons as possible under the term "clergy." For example, all such orders as Templars, Hospitallers, lay brethren known as Beghini or *Fratres Gaudentes* or the Order of Altopascio [1] and

---

[1] *et eos qui de alto passu.* This puzzling description doubtless refers to the lay mendicant Order of Altopascio, the seat of which was in Tuscany on the border between Florence and Lucca. The Rule of this Order is printed in the collection called *Curiositá Letterarie*, vol. liv, Bologna, 1864. The Italian manuscript, supposed by the editor to be a translation from a Latin original made about 1300, gives the name as Altopasso. This plainly suggests the derivation, *altus passus*. It is, therefore, quite intelligible that a branch of the Order established in Paris by King Philip IV (1285–1314) should have been called *du Haut Pas*. The use of this name seems to have caused the original Altopascio entirely to disappear. It does not occur in the description of the Hospital of the Order in Paris given in Du Breul, *Théâtre des Antiquitez de Paris*, 1612, nor in Helyot, *Histoire des Ordres Religieux et Militaires*, ii, 282, 2d ed. 1792. In both cases the

so on *pro libito*. If all persons of this sort are to be exempted from the jurisdiction of civil rulers, with immunity also from public burdens, it seems a very obvious danger that the greater part of mankind may slip into these orders. If this should happen the coercive jurisdiction of rulers would be left without effect, a grave evil and corruption of the republic. "For whoever enjoys the honors and advantages of a civil community, as, for example, the peace and protection of the human Lawgiver, should not be exempted from its burdens and its jurisdiction without the action of the Lawgiver itself. "To avoid this we must admit, in accordance with the Truth, that the ruler has jurisdiction over all bishops or presbyters and clergymen by authority of the Lawgiver, in order that the republic may not go to pieces through undue multiplicity of powers. The ruler ought further to assign a certain number of clergymen to each district subject to him, as also of every other class of citizens, lest through their undue increase they come to resist the coercive power of the ruler or otherwise to disturb the peace of the realm and impede the community or the kingdom in carrying out its necessary activities."

In the effective sense of the word "judge," there is but one who can give final judgment as to transgressions of the divine law, that is Christ and no other. In this world there is no judge who can exercise coercive jurisdiction for such offences. The priest is, so far as this world is concerned, only a "doctor," or expert. His business is to teach, to exhort, to convince by argument, to terrify transgressors by fear of future condemnation at the judgment seat of Christ, but not to compel by force. Such enforced conformity is of no use whatever, since it profits nothing to the man so far as his eternal salvation is concerned. So that, "in accordance with the Truth and the obvious inten-

origin of the Order is said to have been at Lucca. It was only the unfailing linguistic instinct of my colleague, Professor George Foot Moore, working downward from Marsiglio's *qui de alto passu* to the French *Haut Pas*, that enabled me to work upward again from this to Altopascio and to discover the missing link in Altopasso. A considerable account of the Order with many documentary proofs is given in Giovanni Lami, *Deliciae Eruditorum*, Florence, 1769, vol. xviii, pp. 50–184. All three of these rare books are in the library of Harvard College.

tion of the Apostle and of those holy men who were the most
famous doctors of the Church, no one is to be compelled in this
world to obey the Gospel law by any form of punishment or
penalty, whether he be a believer or an unbeliever.   Consequently, no minister of this law, bishop or presbyter, can judge
any one in this world (in the third sense of the word 'judgment'), nor compel any one to observe the divine law, especially without the authority of the human Lawgiver."

We are thus led naturally to Marsiglio's views as to the
punishment of heretics.   He does not question that the heretic
deserves some kind of correction, and admits that at first
thought such correction seems to be the function of the priest
as the expert in the divine law.   But here comes in his fundamental distinction again.   It is Christ alone who can judge the
heretic for his offence against the divine law, and this judgment
is reserved for the world to come.   If, however, he be forbidden
to remain in the region where his heresy was proven, then, as a
transgressor of human law he may be coerced by the custodian
of that law, as authorized by the human Lawgiver.   But if the
human law allows him to stay in the community of the faithful, then "I say that no one has the right to coerce the heretic
or other infidel by any penalty or punishment, real or personal,
so far as his status in this life is concerned.   The reason for this
is a general one: that no one, however he may sin in matters of
opinion, is to be punished or coerced in this world for the
opinion itself, but only in so far as he offends against a command of the human law."

Marsiglio next devotes several chapters to the critical question of apostolic poverty and its modern application in the form
of sacerdotal poverty.   Nowhere else does he let himself go in
bitter accusation of the folly and wickedness of the clergy as
he does here.   As usual he begins with definitions, analysing
with the utmost care the various forms and degrees of property
rights in a civil society.   Especially interesting in view of the
later exposition by Wycliffe and his followers is Marsiglio's
definition of *dominium* or lordship.   "Strictly, *dominium*
means supreme control over a thing justly acquired and so held
that no one else has a right to this thing without the express

consent of the person in control." In common usage this definition applies, not only to a thing itself, but to the use or usufruct of the thing, a distinction which underlies the most important of Wycliffe's contentions on this subject. Marsiglio, however, does not here enlarge upon this point, but includes both kinds of *dominium* in his later applications. The term applies to ownership by corporations as well as individuals, and this gives the opportunity for references to the property of religious orders. "We must not forget" says our author, "that there are some of the voluntary poor who have abandoned earthly things from honorable motives and in suitable ways. But there are others who seem to have given up these things not with any such purpose but for vain glory or some other wordly deceit (*fallaciam*). We must bear in mind also that of earthly goods (which they call riches) there are some which according to ordinary human needs are to be consumed at once, as food, drink, medicine and the like; others of a permanent kind which by their very nature serve many uses, as land, houses, tools, clothing, horses and slaves."

As a conclusion from this distinction Marsiglio lays down what seem to him sound principles of sacerdotal economy. Clergymen should be content with their daily bread and the necessary clothing if they desire to attain a condition of perfection or poverty in the highest sense (*summam paupertatem*). But on the other hand it is the bounden duty of those to whom they minister to supply these necessities if they are able to do so, and the clergyman has the right to demand such support, though not by coercive process in this present life. He can have recourse only to the "divine law." There is no warrant in Scripture for requiring tithes or any other part of the property of the faithful. If the community is so poor that it cannot support the clergy, then they must seek some other honorable and suitable way of increasing their income.

"Now someone will ask, to whom belongs the *dominium* or right of suit before a civil court over such temporalities and especially over real property, since, as we have shown, such *dominium* does not belong to gospel ministers in their state of perfection. I say, that the ownership of property set apart

for the maintenance of ministers of the Gospel belongs to the
Lawgiver or to its deputies for this special purpose appointed
either by the Lawgiver or by the donors of such property.
Persons thus appointed for the defense and recovery of ecclesiastical property are usually called "patrons" of churches. . . .
It is not fitting, therefore, that Christ's perfect ones, the
successors of the apostles, should reserve to themselves fields,
towns, or fortresses.   Never was there given in the acts or the
example of Christ a formula to the Church for holding lordship
over real property or of reserving it to themselves for the future,
but examples of the opposite we do indeed find in Scripture.
A formula for holding personal property for the purpose above
specified we do find, but nowhere for holding real property."

It is at this point that Marsiglio strikes hands with the
Spiritual Franciscans in their crusade for the evangelical
poverty of the clergy and especially in their fight against Pope
John XXII.   In thus making common cause with a class of
persons as little likely as any to be accused of unorthodoxy his
case was greatly strengthened.

VII

Marsiglio is now prepared to move on to the most telling
argument in his whole attack, and to grapple with the vital
question of papal supremacy.   By way of introduction he
summarizes once more what he has already laid down as to the
nature of the sacerdotal office.   His main distinction here is
between the essential quality or "character" of the priest and
his other more distinctly functional quality.   The former includes the power to celebrate the sacrament of the Eucharist
and to absolve the faithful from their sins.   This power is
granted by God through Christ immediately, though with a
certain preparatory human ceremony, as the laying on of
hands and the utterance of certain words.   These human acts,
however, have no effect in so far as the conferring of the essential sacerdotal character is concerned, although "they precede
in pursuance of a certain divine covenant or ordinance."
"Quite another thing is that human institution by which one

priest is set above others, or by which priests are assigned to certain territories for the instruction of the peoples in the divine law, for administering sacraments and dispensing those temporal rights which we call "church benefices." As regards the former, the essential priestly character, all priests are equal as all the Apostles were equal. No one of the Apostles had authority over any other or over the whole body of them, either as to their essential and primary character or as to any secondary institutions.

In this way Marsiglio leads up to the vital question of the Petrine supremacy. We recall that he said rather early that the claim of the Roman bishop to supremacy over other elements of the Church had in recent times been shifted from the historical basis of the Constantinian Donation to the dogmatic or speculative basis of the Petrine succession. This has, therefore, become the very crux of the whole papal position and is in consequence selected by Marsiglio as the most critical point in his attack. Taking up the argument as to the equality of the priestly character he applies it at once directly to Peter.

"Peter had, therefore, no power and still less any coercive jurisdiction directly from God over the other apostles, neither the power of inducting them into the sacerdotal office, nor of setting them apart, nor of sending them out on their work of preaching, excepting that we may fairly admit a certain precedence over the others on account of age or service (*officio*) or perhaps from circumstances (*secundum tempus*) or the choice of the apostles, who properly revered him — although no one can prove such a choice from Scripture. The proof that what we are saying is true is, that we find in Scripture that St. Peter assumed no peculiar authority for himself over the other apostles, but, on the contrary maintained an equality with them. For the whole body (*congregatio*) of the Apostles was of higher authority than that of Peter alone or of any other Apostle. Why, then, do certain sacrilegious flatterers take upon themselves to say that any one bishop has from Christ plenitude of power over clergymen, not to say over laymen, when neither Peter nor any other Apostle ever presumed to ascribe such power to himself either by word or deed?" ....

"Furthermore, since it is written that Peter was elected bishop at Antioch by the multitude of the faithful, not needing the confirmation of the other Apostles, and that the rest of the Apostles presided over other regions without the knowledge of Peter or any institution or confirmation by him (since they were sufficiently consecrated by Christ), we ought in the same way to hold that the successors of these Apostles needed no confirmation from the successors of Peter. Nay, more, that many successors of other Apostles were duly elected and installed as bishops and governed their provinces as holy men without any further institution or confirmation by the successors of Peter."

As to the supremacy of the bishop of Rome as the successor of Peter, it is marvellous, says Marsiglio, that people will overlook the fact that the Roman bishops are the successors rather of Paul than of Peter, and it is "supermarvellous" when we consider that it is not the See of Rome but the See of Antioch which ought justly to claim this succession. It was Paul who was sent out to preach the Gospel to the Gentiles, as Peter was sent to the Jews. "It can be proved by Scripture that Paul was two years at Rome, preached there and converted all Gentiles who were willing to be converted, and therefore it is evident that he was in a special sense bishop of Rome and exercised there the pastoral office, having his authority from Christ, commanded thereto by revelation and elected by the consent of the other Apostles." "But, as to Peter, I say that it cannot be proved by Scripture that he was bishop of Rome or, what is more, that he was ever at Rome. For it seems most amazing if, according to some popular saint's legend, St. Peter came to Rome before St. Paul, preached there the word of God and was then taken prisoner, if then St. Paul after his arrival in Rome acting together with St. Peter had so many conflicts with Simon Magus and in defence of the faith fought against emperors and their agents, and if finally, according to the same story, both were beheaded at the same time for their confession of Christ, there fell asleep in the Lord, and thus consecrated the Roman Church of Christ — most amazing, I say, that St. Luke, who wrote the Acts of the Apostles and Paul himself make not the slightest mention of St. Peter."

When Paul came to Rome the Jews there declared that they knew nothing about this "new sect" except that it was everywhere badly spoken of (Acts xxviii, 22). Now, asks Marsiglio, can any one who is seeking the truth and not merely looking for an argument believe that Peter had come to Rome in advance of Paul and had not said a word about Christ? Or that Paul, if he had known that Peter had been preaching there would not have referred to him as a witness? "Can any one think that Paul was for two years with Peter at Rome and had no intimate relations with him, for, if he had, that the author of the Acts would not have mentioned it? For in other and less important places where Paul met Peter he mentions him, as at Corinth and at Antioch and many other places, and if he had met him at Rome, the most important city in the world, where, according to the above story St. Peter was in charge as bishop, how could he have failed to mention him? So that these things are practically (*quasi*) incredible, and that story or legend cannot with any probability be accepted as to this part of it, but must be reckoned among the apocryphal writings. But according to Scripture it ought to be held without a doubt that Paul was bishop of Rome, and if some one else was with him at Rome, nevertheless Paul should for the above reasons be regarded as the sole and chief Roman bishop, while Peter should be considered as bishop of Antioch, as is evident in the second chapter of the letter to the Galatians. I do not deny that Peter was bishop of Rome, but I hold it to be very probable that in this he did not precede but rather followed Paul."

The Petrine legend is thus, so far as the essence of it is concerned, thoroughly demolished. Marsiglio, like any fair minded Protestant controversialist, is willing to admit the great probability of Peter's presence in Rome and even that he may have had some such leadership in the Christian community there that he may fairly be described as its "bishop." What he will not admit for a moment is that he was in any special sense designated in any way as the divinely ordained head of the Roman Christians. Still less will he admit that, whatever leadership Peter may have had at Rome, this was of such a nature as to give to his successors there any shadow of a right over the successors of the other Apostles in their several districts.   In so far as the papal supremacy rests upon the Petrine argument, the author of the *Defensor Pacis* rejects it absolutely.   Never, in the hottest controversies of the Reformation period was this line of attack followed more completely or more convincingly.   Never, with all the resources of modern scholarship has anything essential been added to the chain of evidence which has shown the weakness of the Petrine claim as the basis of papal supremacy.   Marsiglio is the pioneer in the use of a strictly historical method in examining the foundations of the imposing structure of the mediaeval church.   We have here no metaphysical speculation and no appeal to formal logic. The Papacy claimed to rest on a series of historical facts; Marsiglio's contribution was to show the instability of these alleged facts.   Other and far more valid grounds for the Roman supremacy there were indeed, but at this point Marsiglio is not concerned with them.   For the moment it is the Petrine question and that alone which holds his attention, and to this he clings with extraordinary consistency until he has disposed of it in all its details.

Quite distinct, as we have already seen, from the essential quality of the priest as the dispenser of divine law to the faithful is the function of assigning specific clergymen to special territories and of determining their relation to the means of support.   Marsiglio now addresses himself to the task of defining more accurately this latter process, in other words of describing the actual and the ideal conditions of the system of benefices that formed the basis of so enormous a part of the curial activities of his day.   From what source did this control of the clerical forces of Christendom originate?   True to his guiding principle Marsiglio declares that in the beginning, especially before the conversion of the nations, the active cause (*causa factiva*) of this secondary determination of place and condition of living was either the whole body of the Apostles or some one of them, as circumstances might dictate.   Then, after the time of the Apostles and the early Fathers, by a certain order of succession and especially in communities that were already completely developed (*jam perfectis*) the immediate active source has been and ought to be either the whole body of the faithful in the given community acting through its own voluntary election, or else the individual or individuals to whom the community has committed authority to carry out such arrangements. Such trustee of the community's interests may be compelled by it to take action or may at its discretion, be removed from office. In well organized communities it is the human Lawgiver alone who has the duty of selecting, prescribing, and presenting the persons who are to be raised to ecclesiastical orders. No priest or bishop alone and no college of priests may assist any one to obtain ecclesiastical rank without permission of the human Lawgiver or of the prince who rules by its authority.

As to the *temporalia* (usually called benefices), Marsiglio reminds us again that these are established either by the community for the support of ministers of the Gospel "and other persons deserving compassion (*miserabiles*)," or else by some individual or corporation. In the former case the Lawgiver alone has the right to appoint and remove officials who shall present to the clerical office. In the latter, this right belongs to the donor or donors, always, however, subject to correction by the Lawgiver in any doubtful case. The climax of this chapter is reached in Marsiglio's doctrine of ecclesiastical taxation. "And again, from what has been said it must be clear that the human Lawgiver or the prince ruling by its authority, in case there is a surplus above the needs of the ministers of the Gospel, arising from ecclesiastical property, especially from real estate, may lawfully collect taxes and revenues therefrom according to both human and divine law, for the defence of the country or the redemption of captives as a service to religion, or for carrying on public works or other reasonable purposes according to the judgment of the Christian Lawgiver. For the grantor of such temporalities to an individual or a corporation for pious uses may not grant them with any greater immunity than they had while they were in his possession. They were not exempt from public burdens then, and cannot be so after their transfer by a donor or founder into the possession of another."

Having thus disposed of the Petrine claim of the Roman bishopric to supremacy over others and so over the Church as a whole, Marsiglio proceeds to examine those other claims which may be summed up in the one word "historical." He cites his authorities, including here especially the collection of canon laws known by the name of Isidore. In his estimate of the authenticity of these authorities he stands on the level of his own time, neither higher nor lower. He accepts, not only the Donation of Constantine with certain reservations, but also the Forged Decretals, now universally admitted to be a fabrication of the ninth century, but then received as undoubted evidence of a certain right of dictation by Rome to the other churches in the period before Constantine. Marsiglio sums up his results as follows:— During the whole of that period no bishop exercised any coercive jurisdiction over other bishops. What happened was, that many bishops in other provinces, when they were in doubt regarding Holy Scripture or the correct practice of the Church, since they did not venture to come together openly, consulted the bishop and the church at Rome. They did this because of the greater number and the greater experience (*peritia*) of the Roman Christians, since the pursuit of all kinds of learning flourished greatly at that time in Rome, and in consequence its bishops and priests were better schooled than those in other places. Furthermore, they were held in greater reverence on account of Peter, the senior of the Apostles, who was said to have been bishop there, and of Paul, of whom the same is even more probable. The same kind of respect was paid to the City of Rome as the capital and most famous city of the world.

These are all practical reasons, historically justified. Marsiglio's implication is plain: if it had been possible for the provincial bishops to come together they would have fallen back upon the fundamental right of the community to determine its rules of practice for itself. In the absence of this possibility, they turned to the most obvious source, the center toward which the provincial looked for direction in all matters of legal or political import. They applied to Rome for suitable directors of their spiritual interests, because such persons abounded at Rome. Their applications were met by the Roman Christians in a spirit of fraternal affection (*charitative atque fraterne*) and bishops were sent out ("though men could scarcely be found who were willing to accept this office"). So also the Roman orders were communicated to the provincial churches, and dissensions among them were heard and disposed of in Christian love. "But now, from this priority of custom and the voluntary acquiescence of the other churches the bishops of Rome went on successively to assume a more ample authority and to issue decretals or ordinances for the whole Church in matters pertaining to church practice and to the conduct of the clergy, down to the time of Constantine. That emperor seems to have exempted the clergy from the coercive jurisdiction of the civil authorities. He seems also to have given to the church of Rome and to its bishop rights and powers over all other bishops and churches, which they now, however, as we have already shown, claim to be derived from another source" (namely, the Petrine succession).

Marsiglio has thus clearly indicated that in so far as the Roman bishopric represents an ancient and honorable tradition of sound doctrine and correct practice, he is ready to admit its claim to the reverence, and, within limits, even to the obedience of Christendom. What he will not admit is any such basis of divine appointment as entitles Rome to unquestioning obedience and, least of all, to any coercive jurisdiction over other bishoprics or over civil powers. In developing this opposition he asks first: — to what writings must the Christian man give absolute acceptance as a condition of salvation? His answer is, that in the first place Holy Scripture is to be assumed as true and accepted with steadfast faith (*firma credulitas*). The same kind of faith is to be given also to such interpretations of Scripture as are declared by a General Council to be valid, because the decision of such a council is inspired by the Holy Spirit and therefore cannot err. On the other hand, no such implicit faith is to be given to any writing in which there is a possibility of human error. This is the weak point (*hoc patiuntur*) of writings emanating from an individual or a restricted corporation (*collegii partialis*). Such writings as experience shows, may be lacking in truth, which is not the case with the canonical Scriptures.   Marsiglio quotes Augustine in confirmation and closes his inquiry thus: "St. Augustine, therefore, understood by canonical writings only those which are contained in the Bible and not the decretals or decrees of the Roman pontiff or of the college of his priests whom they call "cardinals," nor any other human ordinances whatsoever concerning human actions or contentions and devised by human ingenuity.   For "canon" means rule or standard, a standard because it is something certain, something that is peculiar to Holy Scripture alone as compared with other writings."

VIII

Where, then, are we to look for such authoritative interpretation of Christian faith and practice as shall secure the Church against those errors and schisms which Marsiglio recognizes as fatal to the essential unity of Christendom?   His answer may fairly be described as the first proclamation in the century long campaign which was to result in the great series of General Councils, whereby the whole structure of the Church was to be essentially modified.   If one seeks a point where Pre-Reformation history may be said to begin, one finds it as distinctly marked here as anywhere.   For it is from this point on that the demand for a council which should be radically different from any of those partial assemblies which in the mediaeval period had claimed universal authority grows more and more insistent.   As Marsiglio's doctrine of the People as the source of law penetrated more deeply and more widely into the consciousness of thinking men, the feeling that this same principle must be extended to the Church as well grew more intense, until it culminated in an irresistible demonstration.

The twentieth chapter of the second book of the *Defensor Pacis* contains Marsiglio's program for a working General Council.   Its monumental importance justifies a more ample treatment than we have given to any other portion of his argument.   The problem of the Council, he says, is the settlement of doubtful and sometimes contradictory opinions of learned men in regard to the divine law.   "I propose to show that the principal authority for such a settlement, be it mediate or immediate, is that of a General Council of Christian men or of the majority of them or of those to whom such authority is deputed by the whole body of believers. The method is this: Let all the more important provinces and communities of the world, according to the determination of their human lawgivers, whether their government be unified or manifold, and in proportion to the number and quality of the inhabitants, select pious men, first priests and then laymen, suitable persons of blameless life and skilled in the divine law. These are to act as judges (in the first meaning of that word), i. e., as experts representing the whole company of believers. They are to assemble in virtue of the authority committed to them by their several communities (*universitates*), in a place selected by the majority of them or of their lawgivers, and there are to settle matters pertaining to the divine law which may appear doubtful, determining what things are useful, what are expedient and what are necessary. They have further to decide with regard to other matters concerning the church ritual or divine worship as shall best conduce to the peace and order of the faithful."

Attendance at the Council is to be obligatory, enforced if necessary by the civil authority. Priests are bound to this duty by the nature of their office; but laymen also, if selected to serve, are equally under obligation to be present and to assist in the discussion of matters affecting the common welfare. Such a council is vested with final authority in the matters presented to it, and this excludes the final authority of "any one single person or college." A proof of the need of lay co-operation at councils is found in the historical fact, that in those of the early Church Christian emperors and empresses with their court officials were present and aided in the settlement of doubtful points. If this was proper then, how much more so now, when the throng of priests and bishops ignorant of the divine law is so much greater. When priests differ among themselves as to what must be believed in order to attain eternal life, the decision must rest with the majority of the faithful.

"If the Pope of Rome or any other single bishop had authority of this sort, or if the letters and decrees of the Roman pontiff were of equal authority with the decisions of a General Council, then all the governments of the world, all kingdoms and provinces and all persons of whatsoever dignity or preeminence or condition, would be subject to the coercive jurisdiction of the Roman bishop. For this is what Boniface the Eighth declared in his letter or decree beginning "*Unam sanctam catholicam ecclesiam*" and ending: "We proclaim, declare and establish, that henceforth it is a necessary article of faith that every human creature is subject to the Roman pontiff." . . . Now, however, it is clear that this is false from the beginning, the most injurious of all imaginable falsehoods to the welfare of all civilized peoples." Its falsity and its folly are shown by the decree "*Meruit*" of Clement V, which expressly exempts the king and people of France from its operation.

In early times matters of doubt could be settled by assemblies of the clergy alone. "Now, however, on account of the corruption of the church administration, the greater part of the priests and bishops are but little versed in sacred Scripture, so that the temporalities of benefices, are gained by greedy and litigious office seekers through servility or importunity or bribery or physical violence. And, before God and the company of the faithful, I have known numbers of priests, abbots, and other church dignitaries of such low quality that they could not even speak grammatically. And what is worse, I have known and seen a man less than twenty years of age and almost completely ignorant of the divine law entrusted with the office of bishop in a great and important city when he not only lacked priestly ordination, but had not passed through the diaconate or subdiaconate."

The General Council thus defined is to be called together by the human Lawgiver and is to act under the special protection and supervision of the ruler who represents the Lawgiver. It is clear, says Marsiglio, that this cannot be the function of the Roman bishop or of the College of Cardinals, because, if he alone or with them were to be accused of crimes requiring the judgment of a council it is highly probable that he would delay calling it, or would put it off entirely to the grave injury of the body of the faithful. This temptation does not exist for the faithful Lawgiver or the community of believers, since they or the majority of them are not easily to be corrupted. Furthermore the enforcement of the conciliar decrees against all offenders, clerical as well as lay, belongs to the human Lawgiver or to his representative, the temporal ruler. This right extends even to making statutes regulating the government of the Holy See and the election of the Roman pontiff. It includes a multitude of details such as fasts, restrictions of marriage within certain degrees of relationship, charters to new religious orders, imposition of penalties in person or property. "For it were a scandal to the peace and order of the community of the faithful if an ignorant or malicious priest or bishop or any college of them should excommunicate a prince or lay an interdict upon a province."

The Council is to be the supreme and final judge in regard to assignments to benefices, the issuing of licenses to teach, notarial commissions and similar grants. If the principle of the "*Unam Sanctam*" were to be enforced, it would mean the gravest danger or even complete ruin to all civil governments. "In his edicts against the noble Ludwig, Duke of Bavaria, accepted as King of the Romans, a certain person called Roman Pope, professes to be dealing only with the Roman kingdom or empire, but in reality he includes all governments, ascribing to himself plenitude of power and thus covering all other kings as well as the prince of the Romans. This bishop, I say, is seeking jurisdiction over all the princes of the earth in order to control the granting of benefices and tithes, and is thus stirring up sedition especially throughout the whole Roman Empire." Hence follows the duty of the human Lawgiver (i. e. the People) and of the prince representing it to watch this whole business of the church temporalities and to see to it that if there is any surplus beyond the needs of the clergy it be devoted to the necessities of the public defence or other service to the community.

The most impressive feature of this conciliar scheme is its **representative character**. It proceeds from the base of the social structure upward to its higher levels, not from above downward.   The unit of representation is the local community acting on the initiative of its own civil authorities.   The delegates, clerical as well as lay, are to act in virtue of the authority derived from the community, not in virtue of any essential quality of their own.   The clerical members, to be sure, have an especial qualification as experts in faith and morals, but only as such.   Their opinions are to command respect only upon their individual merits.   Even the selection of the place of meeting, always a consideration of great importance, is to be in the hands of the delegates themselves or of their constituent communities, an obvious precaution against "packing" by any centralized authority.   The choice of delegates is to rest partly upon a numerical basis, partly upon that established distinction of social classes which no rational scheme of reform in the fourteenth century could wholly ignore.

It is in this matter of the General Council that the intellectual kinship of Marsiglio and William Ockham is most clearly manifest.   In Ockham's most famous treatise, the Dialogue [1] between an inquiring Scholar and a somewhat appallingly learned but affectedly reluctant *Magister* written about 1340 we have an elaborate discussion of the nature and powers of the Council analogous at almost every point with that of Marsiglio.   As the latter bases his argument upon the fundamental right of the whole body of citizens to act immediately and directly in matters of interest to all, so Ockham, the professional champion of the new philosophy of Nominalism, starts with the conception of a state or of a church as an aggregate of individuals, bound together indeed by common interests, but not thereby divested of their essential individual quality.

An illustration of this principle and at the same time of Ockham's logical method is found in his discussion of the question whether a General Council can fall into error in a matter of faith.   (Dial., Part I, Book iii, ch. 25).   "Individuals, liable to error when they were in divers places, continue to be

[1] *Dialogus Magistri Guillermi de Ockam doctoris famosissimi*, in Goldast, *Monarchiae S. Romani Imperii etc.*   Frankfurt, 1668. II, pp. 392–957.

so liable when they come together in one place. Their coming together does not prevent some of them from being perverted in their faith (*inobliquabiles*). For, as the place does not sanctify the man, so the place can confirm no man in his faith. . . . If a hundred or two hundred bishops were (formerly) liable to fall into heresy through their own wills, they could do the same after coming together."

Ockham plays with this argument, twisting it back and forth with every possible device of logic through page after page until he finally forces it to its logical outcome. The General Council may err; the pope and the cardinals may err; is it possible that the whole body of Christians should fall into error? The Scholar asks the question, and the *Magister* replies: "Well, Jews, Saracens, and Pagans firmly believe that the Christian faith is erroneous." "But I wasn't asking for their opinion," replies the Scholar, "I meant to ask whether any Christians believe this, and among Christians I include also heretics."

Mag. "I never heard of a Christian who believed this."

Sch. "And yet, perhaps you could think up some reasons for such an opinion."

Mag. "A false question can be answered only by sophistical reasoning."

Sch. "True; but oftentimes false propositions can be supported by reasons that are plausible and hard to controvert. So, will you kindly try to invent some of these?"

The *Magister* then goes on to say, that one reason why all Christians might fall into error is, that belief, whether of the individual or of the group, is not self-evident but is a matter of will, and the human will is always liable to error. Another reason is as follows: "No one can deny that all Christians excepting two bishops might become heretics. Now, these two bishops might fall into heresy, because God can have no greater care for them than he had for our first parents, and he permitted them to lapse from the faith. Finally, it is clear that any aggregate (*illa multitudo*) of Christians might err, provided only that Christ's promise that his faith should abide forever be preserved inviolate. Now, if all living Christian men and women should become heretics, still this promise would be preserved through the aggregate of baptized children."

Sophistical reasoning indeed! And yet, however fantastic this game of logic-chopping may appear to us, it certainly expresses the very essence of that new mental attitude of which William Ockham was the chief exponent. In the last resort it was no single official or college or assembly or class or sex or age that could give a final verdict in a matter of faith. All these might fail; but even so, somewhere within the body of Christians must be found that mystical witness to the truth which should ensure its permanence.

In spite of Ockham's metaphysical conclusion that no specific portion of the faithful is exempt from error, he recognizes the General Council as practically the efficient representative of the Church as a whole. There was a time, says the *Magister*, when the Church was so small that its members could all come together. Now that this is impossible the next best thing is to secure a true representation. "Therefore, if the several parts of the Church universal elect certain delegates to come together to take action in regard to the Church of God, these delegates in their assembly,— even though there be no lawful pope — may be called a General Council." The method of convening such a Council may be as follows: "Let each parish or other community which can conveniently hold a meeting send one or more persons to a synod of the diocese or to the court (*parlamentum*) of the king or prince or other civil government, and these shall choose delegates to the General Council. Those who are thus chosen by the diocesan or "parliamentary" councils, coming together, may be called a General Council."

Ockham admits that, as a rule (*regulariter*) a true council cannot be called without the authority of a pope; but, if the pope be heretical, or the cardinals fail to choose a new one, then the primitive right of the Church to act re-asserts itself. "Papal authority is never to be interpreted to the prejudice of the Christian faith, for that is superior to any pope, even to a catholic one." As to membership in the Council, Ockham like Marsiglio insists upon the participation of laymen, but goes beyond him in at least apparently advocating the admission of women. He touches the point briefly and with a shade more than his usual caution (c. 85): "The participation of women is defended on the ground of the identity of the faith in men and women, which includes all and in which is neither male nor female. Therefore, where the wisdom, the gentleness (*bonitas*), and the strength of women are necessary to a consideration of the faith, women are not to be excluded from a General Council."

IX

In what sense then, if in any, would Marsiglio accept the headship of any one church or any one bishop over others? He answers this question in detail in the twenty-second chapter of his second book. Unity is essential to the well-being of the Church. This unity can best be secured through a unified administration. A single headship is, therefore, advisable; but of what sort and under what limitations? Marsiglio gives four possible interpretations of the principle of headship. *First*, in such sense that all utterances of the accepted head must be received by all believers as necessary to salvation. *Second*, that all clergymen or colleges of them are subject to the coercive jurisdiction of the supreme pontiff. *Third*, that he or his special college has the sole right of assigning benefices and distributing their emoluments. All three of these conceptions of supreme pontifical right Marsiglio has already discussed and rejected *in toto*.

There remains a fourth, the details of which are laid down at considerable length. According to this view, the basis of any single headship of the Church is to be found in the approval of a General Council or of the human Lawgiver. The functions of the Head, who is always to act in accord with a college of priests assigned to him for this purpose by the Lawgiver or by a General Council, are as follows: *First*, to notify the Lawgiver whenever a case is brought before him of such importance that it seems to require the action of a council, in order that the summons to the council may be duly issued by the Lawgiver as set forth above. *Second*, to "hold the chief place at the council." (Whether this implies a presidency in the modern sense, may perhaps be questioned.) He is to propose topics for discussion, to direct the drawing up and certifying of the record of proceedings, to communicate the result to any churches which may so request, and to make himself master of the decisions so that he can give instructions in regard to them. He is to punish their violation with spiritual penalties, but always under direction of the council and without recourse to any coercive action against persons or property. He, together with a majority of the college assigned to him by the council, may sit in judgment upon bishops or churches in strictly spiritual matters, but always with a right of appeal to the human Lawgiver or to the General Council.

In this sense, and in this alone, Marsiglio thinks, the headship of a single bishop and church over others is expedient for the Church as a whole. But what church and which bishop shall it be? Speaking according to the strictest truth, it ought to be that bishop who excels others in purity of life and in sacred learning, and it ought to be that church which most abounds in men of the highest character and most brilliant accomplishment in sacred things. But, other things being equal or not greatly different, it is the church of Rome which comes nearest this ideal standard. Again Marsiglio reviews the actual or historical claims of Rome to leadership among the churches and finds them valid. As before he yields not an inch to the idea of apostolic succession. It is not the Petrine claim, but the reverence for the memory of Peter and Paul, the greatness of Rome the City, her purity of doctrine and her Christian charity toward other and weaker communities, that make the solid foundations of her acknowledged headship. To these was added the legalisation of Constantine's gift to make the structure complete. In that gift lay also implicit the right of the civil power to control the action of the ecclesiastical headship it had thus sanctioned. As the basis of civil power is found in the sovereign people represented by its rulers, so the final control over the action of the ecclesiastical head is vested in the General Council, whose protector and representative is the civil executive. It is clear, therefore, that the human Lawgiver has the final authority to discipline the head of the

Church and ultimately to depose him if he abuse his power.

With somewhat wearisome iteration Marsiglio recapitulates his version of the expansion of the Roman claims from a simple headship of honor to the *plenitudo potestatis* of the *"Unam Sanctam"*: "This doctrine has been expressed by Boniface the Eighth among other Roman bishops in language as insolent as it is harmful and contrary to the meaning of Scripture, and based upon metaphysical demonstrations. He has gone so far as to decree that the acceptance and confession of this power is necessary to salvation. And this opinion has been followed by his successors, Clement V, and the immediate successor of this Clement, a person called John, although they seem to apply it only to the empire of the Romans. But if they rest, as they say they do, upon the gift of this plenitude of power by Christ, then it is evident that it applies to all the kingdoms of the earth just as much as the power of Christ himself does."

What then is this *plenitudo potestatis* on which the modern Papacy bases its control of all ecclesiastical life in the widest extension of that term? In answering this question Marsiglio indulges once again his passion for accurate definition. He proposes eight possible meanings rising from a simple jurisdiction in spiritual matters to that absolute authority which belongs to the words of Christ alone. All these meanings he rejects as sufficiently covered by what he has already said as to the real nature of papal sovereignty. Only in the sense of a priority or leadership (*principalitas*) over other priests will he admit the use of the phrase at all. What really interests him here as elsewhere is what ought specially to interest us, namely the historical process by which the claim to plenitude of power has actually established itself.

He is ready to accept from the beginning what he calls a *cura animarum generalis*, a general oversight of the spiritual life of Christendom. Thereupon followed — perhaps for gain — a claim to the power of absolution, then the practice of issuing decrees as to ritual observances. Then the imposition of fasts and other restrictions upon the laity as a means to avert calamities, and with this the proclamation of punishments for violation of such restrictions — and all this under the guise of pious

ceremonial. "But then the appetite for wider domination grew
with its own increase. Devoted believers began to be terrified
by language of this sort on account of their low condition and
their ignorance of the divine law. They imagined that they
were bound by whatever their priests might tell them, and so,
through fear of damnation, bishops of Rome together with their
coterie (*coetu*) of clergymen ventured to issue certain despotic
edicts touching upon civil affairs. In these they declared
themselves and the clerical order, including some mere laymen,
exempt from public burdens. They advanced to the clerical
office even married laymen, who were easily allured by the
prospect of enjoying immunity from their obligations to the
State."

Hereupon followed the practice of visiting with excommunication all who attacked in any way the persons of clergymen,
and of calling upon the civil authorities to enforce these spiritual
penalties by the secular arm. And the worst part of this practice was that this process of excommunication was extended to
cover all cases of failure to pay moneys due at a certain date,
thus shutting out from the holy sacraments "those whom Christ
and the blessed Apostles had brought into the Church with pain
and labor and the shedding of their precious blood."

"And, not content with this, reaching out after the utmost
limit of secular power, they have broken out (*proruperunt*) into
legislation quite apart from that of the civil community,
declaring the whole clergy exempt from civil jurisdiction and
thus bringing about political divisions and an impossible multi-
plication of supreme rule. The realm of Italy is the root and
origin of this pestilent condition. There the whole scandal had
its germ and its development and as long as this continues there
will be no end of civil disorders. For this power, which he
gradually and with sly deception crept into, the Roman bishop,
of late through custom, or rather through abuse, has seized
upon and, fearing that he will be deprived of it by the Prince
[i. e. the emperor] as he well deserves to be, on account of the
excesses he has committed, he prevents the election and inaugu-
ration of the Prince of the Romans with every kind of malicious
interference. A certain one of them has gone so far in his

insolence as to proclaim formally that the Prince of the Romans is bound to him by a feudal obligation and subject to his coercive jurisdiction . . . Such despotic ordinances the bishops of Rome and their cardinals dared not call 'laws,' but gave them the name 'decretals,' although they intended them to have binding coercive force in this world just as human law-makers do. They were afraid to use the word 'laws' at first, dreading the resistance and correction of the lawmaking power and the charge of treason against rulers and legislators. From the beginning they called these 'canonical rights' (*jura canonica*) in order to impress the faithful with their validity and to secure their acceptance, their reverence and their obedience."

Such is the nature of that plenitude of power upon which the extraordinary hold of the Roman See upon the church life of the western world was based. It remains to notice some of the consequences as Marsiglio saw them in the political and social conditions of his day. Here, as always, he reverts to his fundamental principle, the right of the whole people to share in the administration of all affairs which concern their welfare. The effect of the *plenitudo potestatis* is, he says, utterly to destroy this principle in the whole field of appointment to cleri-cal offices. The only safe method of securing suitable officials of any sort is by election; but now election has been practically abolished within the Church. It has been restricted by placing it solely in the hands of clergymen. It has been corrupted by leaving episcopal elections to the so-called "canons," a narrow group of young men ignorant of the divine law, to the exclusion of the other clergy of the diocese. It has been crushed out by the system of papal reservations extending even to the lowest offices of the Church. "Through these reservations elections of suitable persons made according to law are quashed, and in their place are thrust ignorant, inexperienced and untrained men, often of corrupt morals or notorious criminals, men who do not even speak the language of those over whom they are placed. . . . If you count them up you will not find one in ten of the provincial archbishops, bishops, patriarchs and the clergy of lower degree who is a doctor of theology or adequately trained in that science." The only kind of persons who can secure appointments are the *causidici,* men skilled in legal quibbling, because they are "useful" in gaining and holding on to the temporalities, whereas the doctors of theology are "useless," simple souls who would allow "the Church" to fall into ruin.

As to the papal elections, these, says Marsiglio, are seldom made from among doctors of theology but rather from the "college of advocates" in shameless disregard of Holy Scripture. The College of Cardinals admits licentious youths unacquainted with sacred learning. This corruption at the center infects the whole body of the Church everywhere. It leads to the appointment of the same kind of persons to the provincial churches. It involves the clergy in political complications, and this brings about the appropriation of church revenues to the maintenance of armies and the continual promotion of quarrels among Christian men.

When Marsiglio speaks of the power exercised over clergymen or laymen by any one single cleric he generally adds "or any *collegium* or *coetus* of them." Such references are obviously to the College of Cardinals. He includes these in his criticisms of the papal maladministration, and evidently thought that some radical measures should be taken to reform them. As to precisely what such reforms should be we get only one constructive suggestion. The root of the evils connected with the cardinalate was the vicious system of appointment. No other electoral system in the whole history of elective governments contained precisely the same element at once of strength and weakness as this. Nowhere else do we find the electoral body appointed by the executive whose successor it was their chief duty to select. We speak loosely of political "rings," but never was there so complete a ring in the literal sense of the word as here. The electoral college of the Empire was a group of territorial lords fixed by the imperial constitution and thus independent of all political influence from the reigning prince. The electors of the Doge in Venice were evolved from a complicated series of more or less freely elected councils always jealous of the ruling executive and his family and ready to supplant them whenever the opportunity should offer. It was only in the papal system that the ring of electors and potential popes was absolutely closed.   The only restraint upon appointment of electors was the individual sense of propriety of the existing pope and the pressure of party politics within and without the limits of the Curia itself.

With Marsiglio may be said to begin the long series of propositions for the reform of this electoral system which continue all through the conciliar period and find their final expression in the Council of Trent.   The essence of all these propositions is the widening of the electorate, the effort to make it more truly representative of the Church as a whole.   Especially was ever increasing emphasis laid upon the necessity of recognizing the growing principle of nationality as the basis of such representation.   In view of the radical suggestions made, for example, at the Council of Constance, going as far even as the abolition of the College of Cardinals, Marsiglio's proposals sound almost conservative.   He aims to break the vicious circle of appointment and election as it was working in his day.   He admits the importance of an advisory council to act with the pope in all official ways, but he would make this board independent of the pope's personal influence.   He would have it appointed by the General Council as the organ of the Church universal.   Whether it should be a permanent board or chosen for specific objects is not quite clear.   In one passage referring to the duty of the pope to notify the *Legislator* of the need of a council Marsiglio says that he shall do this together with his college of priests whom the Lawgiver or the General Council shall have seen fit to associate with him *ad hoc*, as if this were a special assignment of councillors for a specific case.   Numerous other references, however, suggest rather a permanent board to be selected either by the emperor or by the General Council as the executive organs of that *universitas fidelium* which is the last resort in all matters of church administration. Although this suggestion was never adopted, and the ancient method of appointment of cardinals by the pope has continued to the present day, still the spirit of it has been more and more recognized in actual practice.   The personnel of the cardinalate has in fact been greatly improved and made to correspond more accurately to the world-wide membership of the Roman communion. If one is willing to overlook the obvious fact of a dominant Italian majority in the present college, one may fairly describe it as a reasonably representative body of catholic Christendom.

The source of all this evil is that the Head undertakes to control the operation of all the members:

"Who would not regard the body of an animal whose limbs were joined directly to its head as a monstrosity useless for its own proper functions? If the hand were fixed directly upon the head it would lack suitable space and would be deprived of strength, of motion, and of effectual action. But this is not so when the fingers are joined to the hand, the hand to the arm, the arm to the shoulder, the shoulder to the neck, and the neck to the head, all by suitable joints, so that the head can give to each member its own proper activity. Thus the whole body receives its appropriate form and is able to perform its normal functions. So is it with the body of the Church and of civil society as well. The universal pastor or the universal prince cannot directly inspect and control the individual actions of every one throughout all the provinces, but if this is to be done decently and adequately he must have the assistance of special representatives and agents. In this way the body of the Church will be well ordered and will grow as it should. But, if we once admit the *plenitudo potestatis* of the Roman pontiff, this whole beautiful order is destroyed; for he absolves the lower prelates and orders from the power, the oversight and the correction of their superiors."

This is Marsiglio's contribution to the continual conflict between the papal and the episcopal powers. It was no new issue. His criticism of papal aggression was the common protest of all right thinking men of his day against the abnormal development of the centralized papal administration as compared with the constantly growing restrictions upon the local authorities of the Church. It was on this point more than any other that the common interests of civil governments and these local church powers became evident. The alignment of parties generally threw the episcopal order on the side of the government and against papal aggression. This had been wonderfully demonstrated in the great fight between the government of France under Philip IV and the Papacy under Boniface VIII. Whatever may be thought as to the political methods of that far from scrupulous king, it is clear that on the whole he carried the French clergy with him in his struggle for French independence of papal dictation. It could almost be said that the Papacy was, for the time, converted into a French institution. All this Marsiglio had seen at close quarters from his academic residence in Paris. It was unquestionably this experience, combined with his own personal traditions of Italian democracy, that gave such vivid color to his presentation of the situation for the benefit of the German Ludwig. The papal *plenitudo potestatis* was the common enemy of every local right. Marsiglio did not overstate the case in saying, that if this were once conceded there was no limit to the aggression that must ensue toward every form of government in both Church and State.

His passionate indictment of the Roman Curia as a sink of bargain-driving scoundrels is not a whit more venomous than many utterances of Dante and Petrarch on the same theme.

"What do you find there but a swarm of simoniacs from every quarter? What but the clamor of pettifoggers, the insults of calumny, the abuse of honorable men? There justice to the innocent falls to the ground or is so long delayed — unless they can buy it for a price — that finally, worn out with endless struggle, they are compelled to give up even just and deserving claims. For there man-made laws are loudly proclaimed; the laws of God are silent or are rarely heard. There are hatched conspiracies and plots for invading the territories of Christian peoples and snatching them from their lawful guardians. But for the winning of souls there is neither care nor counsel."

Marsiglio's attacks upon the morals of the Curia are of quite secondary importance; for the answer to such criticism is always ready. Evils are to be expected in all institutions administered by human beings. The remedy is to bring the administration into better hands. This is always the watchword of "reform within the party"; improve the adminis-

tration and the evils will take care of themselves. What
Marsiglio's criticism meant was, that the real evil was not
found in the irregularities he enumerates, but in the system
itself. Only by a thoroughgoing reform of the system at the
root of which was the doctrine of *plenitudo potestatis*, could
Christian societies be safeguarded against unlimited abuse of
power. Marsiglio insists over and over again that the cause
of the emperor in his controversy with Pope John XXII is the
cause of all civil governments; but he is, of course, especially
concerned with showing the far-reaching consequences of the
papal claims in the sphere of imperial rights.

Here again he brings the issue down to the essential test, to
the question of the basis of the emperor's claim upon the
allegiance of his subjects. The Empire was the most noteworthy illustration of his fundamental theory of the origin of
all civil jurisdiction. It was an elective institution, perpetu-
ated by the direct action of a limited electorate, but in its theory
that electorate represented the people as a whole. In the
formal statements of the electoral process, beginning with the
Sachsenspiegel in 1230 (?) and closing with the Golden Bull of
1356, after the enumeration of all the individual electors there
follows an express declaration that all the leading men (*die
vorsten alle*) are to express their approval of the choice made by
the college of seven. These leading men come as near to being
the "People" of Marsiglio's theory as mediaeval conditions
could permit. Furthermore, if we assume the year 1324 as the
date of the *Defensor Pacis* it was only two years since the
emperor Ludwig, after eight years of fighting, had maintained
the verdict of the electoral college against the "claims" of the
Habsburg candidate supported by the unwearied activity of
John XXII. We can, therefore, quite understand the vehe-
mence with which Marsiglio makes the application of his argument against the *plenitudo potestatis* to the question of the
imperial electoral right.

"For if the authority of the king elect were dependent solely
upon the will of the Roman bishop the function of the electors
would be absolutely an empty one, since the man whom they
might choose would neither be nor be called "king" until he

should be confirmed by the papal will or the authority of the
so-called Apostolic See, nor could he exercise any royal authority.   He could not even draw from the revenues of the kingdom enough for his daily subsistence without the approval of
that bishop, a thing intolerable and unheard of.   What then
would be the force of an election by the princes beyond that of
a nomination, the final determination of which would depend
upon the will of one other single individual?   Why!   Seven
barbers or seven blind men could convey as much of a sanction
to the King of the Romans as this!   I say this in derision, not
of the electors, but of him who would deprive them of their
due authority.   For he does not understand the force and the
theory of an election, nor why it is that its validity rests upon
the majority (*valentiore parte*) of those to whom the right of
election belongs.   Nor does he realize that the effect of the
election ought not and cannot be dependent upon the will of
any one person, if it is conducted according to rule, but upon
the Lawgiver alone over whom the (elected) ruler is to be
placed, or upon those alone to whom the Lawgiver shall have
entrusted this commission.   The Roman bishop, therefore,
plainly desires to destroy the office of the electors, no matter
how much he may try to blind them and defraud them."

The supreme test of this claim to control over the Empire is
seen at times of vacancy in the imperial office.

"Since the afore-mentioned bishop claims the right to take
the place of the emperor during a vacancy, it follows of necessity that he claims also the right to compel all princes and
feudatories of the Empire to take oaths of allegiance to him.
Furthermore he demands the privilege of collecting all tributes
and other forms of taxation regularly due to the emperor and,
besides these, other exceptional taxes imposed according to the
will of that bishop in virtue of his self-constituted *plenitudo
potestatis*. . . .   The very worst and most dangerous thing of all
is, that thus during an imperial vacancy, which, at the will of
Roman bishops may become perpetual, all princes, associations, communities and individuals under the Empire, in case
of civil suits among themselves are compelled to bring their
suits, real as well as personal, by appeal or by delation to the

court of the Roman bishop and subject themselves to his civil jurisdiction."

The absurd claim that this control over the imperial power is necessary in order to prevent the election of an heretical emperor is disproved by the obvious fact that the electoral college contains three important archbishops who "have received from Christ a sacerdotal and episcopal sanction equal to that of the Roman pontiff." The chance of a bad selection is less among seven electors than if the choice were in the hands of the Roman bishop alone. The intention of these people, says Marsiglio, is none other than to cut the very root of all civil allegiance. "For, in my opinion, the root and bond of this allegiance consists in the mutual and sworn faith of princes and peoples. This faith is, as Cicero says, the foundation of all justice. He who tries to break this bond between rulers and subjects is aiming at nothing less than to overturn the power of all governments and subject them to his arbitrary will."

What then is the remedy? In the answer to this question we have Marsiglio's constructive teaching. All his theoretical arguments are here brought to a focus in a series of practical suggestions: "For these reasons it is advisable that a General Council should be summoned by all princes and peoples after the manner I have recommended. This council should absolutely forbid the use of this term *plenitudo potestatis* by the Roman bishop or any other person whomsoever, that the people may not be led astray through long continued hearing of false things. The Roman bishop should be deprived of all power of conferring ecclesiastical office and of distributing the temporalities or benefices; for that bishop now abuses these powers to the injury of the bodies and the damnation of the souls of the faithful. The duty of calling a council is an obligation resting upon all rulers, especially upon kings according to the law of God. To this end they were instituted: to do justice and give judgment, and failing in this they are without excuse because they well know what scandals will follow upon their neglect."

Here Marsiglio draws a moving picture of the ills that have already befallen his beloved Italy in consequence of the false conditions he has described and closes with this eloquent appeal: "Who, then, would be so brutish a son of this father and mother land, once so beautiful, now so torn and defiled, as to be silent and withold his spirit from crying to the Lord when he sees and knows these things and is able to act against those who rend and betray her?   Verily, as the Apostle says, "he hath denied the faith and is worse than an unbeliever."

The last three chapters of the second '*Dictio*' are devoted to a refutation of the specific arguments in defence of the doctrine of '*plenitudo potestatis.*'   They do not contain any noteworthy addition to the arguments already put forward by Marsiglio on the other side of the controversy.   Most significant is the renewed insistence upon a sound method in the use of authorities.   Supreme above all others is the authority of Scripture, and this is to be interpreted according to the principle of common sense.,   Where no mystical meaning is involved the literal sense of language is to be accepted.   Where a mystical interpretation is required, "I will accept the more probable opinion of holy men.   If, however, they advance opinions of their own, I will accept those which are in harmony with the canon of Scripture.   Those which are discordant with Scripture I will reverently reject, but never without the support of Scripture upon which I shall always rely."

Here is the proclamation of those principles of biblical authority and interpretation which underlie the activities of all the great leaders of the Reformation from Wycliffe to Calvin. In this doctrine of Scripture is to be found, contrary as it seems to all the implications of present day thought, the very essence of modern religious liberty.   It does not imply, as is so often charged upon it, the "slavery to a book" which must lead men into a bondage worse even than that of an infallible church. For after all, every Scripture must be interpreted, and it is in this process of interpretation that modern liberty has worked itself out in the field of religion as everywhere else.   The struggle was to be a long and bitter one, but the key-note had been sounded, and it was never again to lapse into silence.

Marsiglio of Padua is the prophet of that new world of thought and action, to which, in default of a better word, we give the name of "modern."   It is the world in which the right of a man to think as he must and to associate himself with others who think, on the whole, as he does is the dominating principle of social organization.

X

The third and final *Dictio* of the *Defensor Pacis* consists of a brief summary of the argument of the whole work in short paragraphs and with continuous reference to specific passages in the previous books.   It furnishes the natural basis for a review of what we may now fairly call Marsiglio's program for Church Reform.   It bears much the same relation to the activities of the conciliar period as that of Luther's Ninety-five Theses to the work of the Protestant Reformation.   It begins where the main body of the book ended, with the doctrine of the supreme authority of Scripture intepreted by the common action of the whole community of the faithful.   In cases of doubt as to what articles of faith are necessary to salvation, the sole power of decision rests with the General Council or a majority of its members (*valentior multitudo*).   No partial *collegium*, and no individual of whatsoever condition has this power of decision.   Dispensation from things prescribed or prohibited or permitted by the law of the New Covenant belongs solely to the General Council or to the human Lawgiver. This Lawgiver is defined as the whole body of citizens or the majority of them.   Decretals or decrees of Roman or any other bishops whomsoever issued individually or collectively without permission from the human Lawgiver cannot bind anyone by temporal penalties.   Only the Lawgiver or its agent can dispense from human laws.

No elective official who derives his authority from election alone requires any further confirmation or approval.   No bishop or priest has, in virtue of his priestly character, coercive jurisdiction over any clergyman or layman.   All bishops are of equal authority through Christ, nor can it be proved by the law of God that, either in matters spiritual or in things temporal, one bishop is higher or lower than another.   In accordance with divine authority and with the consent of the human

Lawgiver, other bishops acting separately or together, may as properly excommunicate the Roman bishop as he may excommunicate them. It is the right of the civil ruler in accordance with the laws of the Christian community to fix the number of churches and of the clergy who are to officiate therein.

The right to summon a council, general or special, belongs solely to the Lawgiver or to one who governs a Christian community in virtue of its authority; and a council summoned in any other way cannot bind any one to observe its decrees. Those who are bound to the perfection of evangelical poverty may have no *dominium* over any property whatsoever, real or personal. Bishops and other ministers of the Gospel have a right to receive from individuals or from the community what is necessary for food and shelter, but they have no right to tithes or any other form of revenue beyond these necessities. The bishop of Rome, as well as every other spiritual minister, ought to be appointed to his office solely by the Christian Lawgiver or the prince ruling by its authority or by a General Council of the faithful on removable tenure, and should be suspended or deposed from his office by the same in case of malfeasance.

Many other conclusions, says Marsiglio, might be drawn from what he has set forth, but he is content to leave the matter here, believing that these will supply a sufficient line of approach (*ingressum*) for the removal of this plague and the cause of it as well. He thus justifies our use of the word "program" for the summary of his opinions here presented. It is not merely a theoretical, or, as we say now-a-days, an "academic" presentation of an argument. It is a call to action. Although written primarily to meet the immediate problems of the emperor Ludwig's stormy administration, the *Defensor Pacis* has a universal application to all civil governments included under the general term "The Christian Commonwealth." Marsiglio's view does not extend beyond this. His whole scheme rests upon the basic idea of the sovereignty of the People, but the people is the *universitas fidelium*, the community of believers. This people is the ultimate Lawgiver. It is represented by the ruler, and this ruler is the *princeps* or the *principans fidelis*, the Christian prince. The personnel of the civil and the ecclesiastical communities is the same. There is no such thing as a church within the community; the church *is* the community in its religious aspect.

This dual community, however, must have its organs of expression, and these are to be most carefully distinguished one from the other. Here was Marsiglio's most delicate problem. He solved it by his careful analysis of the difference between "character" in the technical sense familiar to every student of church institutions and "function" in the obvious meaning of administrative action. The priestly "character," of divine ordination and conferred through certain sacred rites, gave the power to grant absolution and to perform the eucharistic sacrifice and nothing else. All beyond this, especially all that had reference to the temporal activities of the clergy, was functional, was instituted by human agencies and was, therefore, to be regulated by human laws. The distinction is as sharp as that between the organic and the functional in the living physical body. Just as any conflict between the two in a living organism brings disaster to the whole, so in the community of social beings any confusion of the two ideas is sure to result in an impaired condition of the whole social organism.

That, we recall, was Marsiglio's starting-point. The curse of society in his day was, as he conceived, the corruption of the Church arising from precisely this kind of confusion. The functional activities of the priestly order had steadily encroached upon the strictly sacerdotal, until there was danger that they would entirely absorb them. What was only functional had come to call itself sacred and to claim the privileges of sacrosanctity. The lay elements of the faithful community had not understood the meaning of this tendency. They had let things drift, but now, in the face of the unparalleled audacities of Boniface VIII and John XXII, they were aroused to the fighting point. The rulers of the earth, one after the other, were coming into conflict with the one power in which these perversions of the true Christian order seemed to be concentrated, the power of the Roman bishop and the *collegium* which he dominated.

Marsiglio's mission, as he understood it, was to point out by the method of historical illustration and sound technical definition, the real nature of this conflict. His historical material was by no means of the best, but his method in using it was sound, and his conclusions from it have borne the test of time. Essentially they have not been changed by the discovery of better materials and the wider experience of modern historical science. Marsiglio is properly scandalized by the atmosphere of moral indifference to which, in common with all good observers of his time, he calls attention. But the gravamen of his attack does not lie in the all too easy field of moral criticism. Atrocities as such play little part in his indictment. The one thing that really interests him is the application to the existing conditions in Church and State of the fundamental principle from which he started, the principle of popular sovereignty.

As that principle guided him in his critical study and in his assault upon the prevailing evil of his time, so it furnished the leading idea in his constructive suggestions. The remedy was to be found in an honest and thorough reorganization of the church administration from the bottom upward. The beginning must be made by the civil authorities because they were the only element of the Christian society fitted to take the initiative. But they must proceed, to use the language of present day reform, by going over the heads of the existing church powers and appealing directly to the People. The instrument of this appeal must be the General Council, and this must be, no longer an assembly of clergymen called at the good pleasure of the centralized papacy, but a truly representative body, built up on lines of territorial and class representation, including laymen and directed through the whole process of its assembling and its deliberations by the highest civil authority. Its decrees must be certified and validated by its own sanctions, and, so far as they were concerned with affairs of this world, must be enforced by the civil power.

In this great popular assembly was vested the true unity of Christendom. For practical purposes, however, a central organ of administration was desirable. To this end the ancient and honorable See of Rome was especially indicated. Marsiglio is ready to go all lengths in his admiration for the splendid traditions of pure doctrine and noble service that made the real claim of Rome to the respect of Christians. Her leadership, founded upon actual historical grounds, might be compatible with his doctrine of popular right. What he could not admit was that this leadership rested upon any ground whatsoever which could make it independent of that final control. Rome must be brought down from its theoretical primacy to its original level as the servant, not the master of the Christian community. According to this conception the bishop of Rome was to be the executive agent of the supreme Council. His very election was to be dependent upon its action; for the electoral body was to be appointed by it and no longer selected by his own free choice.

Now, it is obvious that however admirable such a constitution of the Church might be, however well adapted to meet the crying needs of the social order, it was not the papal constitution. Its Head, however dignified and useful, was not a pope. The specifically Roman character of the whole institution was gone. The Petrine tradition which gave and gives still the quality of a divine commission to the authority of the Roman bishop, was shattered. In place of all this was to be a rather vague universalism lacking in all the heroic, the dramatic, and the emotional elements that worked so powerfully in the Roman appeal.

It remains to notice very briefly the fate of the *Defensor Pacis* and its influence upon the development of political theory and practice. Almost immediately after its presentation to the emperor it seems to have become rather widely known to both friends and enemies. Papal condemnations followed in rapid succession, while on the other hand the imperial lawyers were employing arguments apparently borrowed from the *Defensor*. Ludwig's whole activity during the fatal years 1327–1328 was little more than the carrying out into practice of Marsiglio's doctrines of a universal elective monarchy resting upon the will of the people. The fantastic performance of an imperial coronation at Rome at the hands of officials representing the *populus romanus*, which in turn represented the *universitas civium* of the Christian commonwealth, was the dramatic but momentary realization of the Paduan's dream. Its almost immediate collapse was the proof, if proof were needed, how far ahead of his time was this prophet of a new era freed from the cramping limitations of the age just drawing to a close.

In the course of Ludwig's tortuous policy of alternate defiance and submission he makes every sort of formal promises to repudiate his evil counsellors, but without ever taking any practical steps to this effect. If Marsiglio survived the Roman fiasco of 1328, there is no reason to believe that he suffered any actual inconvenience from his repeated condemnations by the Papacy or from the feeble protestations of his imperial patron.

It is, however, quite intelligible that other and later writers on the same or related topics should have been cautious about using the name of a thrice condemned heretic to support their own opinions, and this may well explain the absence of specific references to Marsiglio in writers who otherwise give every indication of knowing his work and of being influenced by it. A notable early indication of this is found in the chief work of Lupold of Bebenburg, bishop of Bamberg, written probably in 1340.[1] In a strictly legal, formal argument Lupold, a canonist of repute, aims to establish the right of the Roman king and emperor as independent of papal sanction. The *translatio imperii* from the Greeks to the German Franks was, to be sure, made by Pope Leo III, but not in virtue of any inherent papal right. It was effected only *casualiter* on a great critical occasion when no other tribunal was entitled to act (c. xii). The electoral right has now become embodied in the college of the German electors. The person elected by them, or by a majority of them, becomes king and administrator of imperial rights in Italy and other provinces subject to the empire. He needs no nomination or confirmation from the pope or from the Roman church. The oath to the pope taken at coronation is not a feudal oath but a pledge of loyal protection. In these doctrines we have the very spirit of Marsiglio's teaching on the same subject. The main purpose of the two

---

[1] *Tractatus de juribus regni et imperii*, ed. Herold, Basel 1562. See also Meyer, H., Lupold von Bebenburg, Studien zu seinen Schriften, 1909.

treatises is the same: the defense of the imperial power against the claims of the Roman See. That the later does not quote the earlier by name cannot obscure the essential similarity of the two. The omission is sufficiently explained by the natural reluctance of the clerical writer to identify himself in any way with so pestilent a controversialist as Marsiglio. Lupold's treatise was the formulation in legal terms of ideas which already two years before, in 1338, had found their practical expression in the enactments of the German Electoral Union at Rense and in the imperial decree *"Licet juris."* The language of these famous documents marks the highest point of the unstable Ludwig's resistance to papal aggression.

If we think of Ludwig as animated throughout by personal hostility to the power which had steadily opposed his most cherished schemes of political and dynastic ambition, we can certainly have no such conception of the man who came to the imperial throne over the ruins of the Bavarian-Wittelsbach policy. Charles IV, the Luxemburg-Bohemian rival and successor of Ludwig, was distinctly the candidate of clerical interests. "King of the Parsons" and "The Pope's Errand-boy" were among the nicknames designed to throw contempt upon this apparent deserter from the true imperial-German cause. And yet, in that monumental document, the "Golden Bull" of 1356, this same Charles IV set his hand to the most positive declaration yet made of the absolute right of the German electoral college to create the King of the Romans and to invest him with all imperial powers without reference of any kind to any outside power whatsoever. The Golden Bull, henceforth to be the corner stone of the German constitution, is the practical embodiment of Marsiglio's theories of a political society.

We have seen that Marsiglio was acutely conscious of the fact, that in championing the cause of imperial independence he was fighting the battle of national integrity everywhere. If, he says, this *plenitudo potestatis* is to be carried out to the consequences already foreshadowed by the aggressive policy of Boniface VIII and John XXII, then every human sovereignty is in danger. How sound this estimate was is clearly shown in the affairs of England. The work of John Wycliffe,

beginning almost at the moment of the publication of the
Golden Bull, was from the first identified with the interests of
English nationality as opposed to foreign clerical domination.
Wycliffe's fundamental proposition, developed in his most
important and most elaborate treatises [1] involved the whole
problem of *"Dominium"* to which we have already referred.
Among the heresies of Marsiglio his views on this subject took a
prominent place.   These views, hardly more than outlined in
the *Defensor Pacis*, were expanded by Wycliffe at portentous
length.   As a political theorist Marsiglio was primarily interested in establishing the right of civil government to a life of
its own independent of any outside control.   Wycliffe, as a
philosopher and theologian, was chiefly concerned with fixing
the conditions of the ecclesiastical order.   He came to the
question of the relation between church and state from the side
of the church.   He saw, more clearly than any one before him,
that the crucial problem was the nature of the Church's right to
deal with the goods of this world as represented by the income
from the vast properties, which under one or another form had
slipped into its administrative control.

In other words he was led to that fundamental distinction
between the *spiritualia* and the *temporalia* which occupied so
important a place in Marsiglio's definition of terms.   The
arguments of the *Defensor* may in this respect be regarded as
prolegomena to Wycliffe's *Dominium*.   So comprehensive is
this word in Wycliffe's thought, that it covers pretty much
the whole range of theological speculation.   The mere possession of earthly goods is but an item in the larger concept of a
rule founded in the order of a divinely controlled universe.
Marsiglio had drawn in sharply cut phrase the basic definition
of the spiritual and the temporal, but he had offered no test by
which in a specific case the right of control over temporal things
was to be determined.

That test it remained for Wycliffe to supply.   He found it in
his doctrine of "Righteousness," the keynote of his whole

---

[1] *Johannis Wycliffe de dominio divino libri tres, ed.* R. L. Poole, 1890.

Johannis Wycliffe tractatus de civili dominio liber primus, ed. R. L. Poole, 1885;
ll. ii-iv, *ed.* J. Loserth, 1900–1904.

theological system. God, he says, as the supreme righteousness, is lord of all things. All other lordship is derived from
this ultimate source. Only the righteous man can be conceived
of as having a right to any lordship at all. If any man fail in
righteousness he, in so far, forfeits his right of lordship. What
had appeared to be such must then be treated as only a limited
right of use, not of absolute ownership. Righteousness, according to Wycliffe, is the state of grace into which a man is brought
by a divine process independent of his own activity. *Dominium*, therefore, is limited to the elect. Any person outside
that body is by this fact deprived of any claim to lordship.

So far we are dealing with speculative, theological definitions,
but when we come to their practical application we leave
theology and enter the realm of hard, work-a-day politics.
The critical problem for Wycliffe as for Marsiglio is found in
the question: Supposing a pope is not among the elect, what
then? Obviously he can have no *dominium*. But, who is to
determine the fact of his unrighteousness? In answering this
question Wycliffe, like all others before and since who have
grappled with it, is obliged to fall back upon the evidence of
personal conduct. If a pope so conduct the business of his
great office as to offend the common sense of Christendom, then
Christendom as a whole has the right to treat him as lacking in
the divine gift of righteousness and may proceed to discipline
him for his offence. Wycliffe's argument here, freed from its
almost impenetrable tangle of scholastic involution, follows
very nearly the lines of Marsiglio's thought. He does not, so
far as I know, refer to him by name, but the resemblance is
unmistakable, and the conclusion is irresistible that Wycliffe
had before him the text of the *Defensor Pacis*.

Thus fairly launched on its career as a reformatory pamphlet
Marsiglio's work penetrates every attempt at church reform
made during the five generations between Wycliffe and Luther.
It came to be one of the stock charges made against every leader
of reform that he was repeating the heresies of Wycliffe and
through him those of Marsiglio. Even though the reformer
himself made no allusion to his fourteenth century predecessor,
and may, indeed, have been more or less unconscious of the

debt he owed him, the sure instinct of the still dominant but now thoroughly frightened Church pointed unerringly to the essential continuity of ideas from Marsiglio onward.

As soon as lists of prohibited writings began to be published the *Defensor Pacis* figured prominently among those of the worst class. Its place in this honorable company was firmly established by the Council of Trent in the *Index librorum prohibitorum* of 1558. During the sixteenth and seventeenth centuries several editions of the *Defensor* appeared in France and Germany, the last at Frankfurt in 1692. The motive back of the earliest editions was mainly hostility to the papal power rather than interest in theories of the state. In the later editions the political motive predominates. This is shown by the incorporation of the *Defensor* in the great collection of Goldast which bears the title: The Monarchy of the Holy Roman Empire or Treatises on the Imperial, Royal and Pontifical Jurisdiction, Frankfurt, 1614–1668.

Every modern writer on political theory has given to Marsiglio some consideration, but seldom a space proportioned to the importance of his work. It is, therefore, a matter of congratulation that the administration of the *Monumenta Germaniae Historica* has decided to publish what is likely to be for a long time to come the definitive text of the *Defensor Pacis* and has entrusted the work to the scholar who appears at present to be best prepared by preliminary studies to undertake it. It is to be hoped that the obscurity which has so long rested on this extraordinary book will at last be lifted and that it will take its rightful place among those forces that have worked most powerfully in the making of the modern world. For the *Defensor Pacis*, made under the stress of a specific conflict remote in time and apparently of slight importance at the present day, yet deals with principles of human organization of permanent and decisive value. In a time like this, when the right of the common man to a voice in the making of the laws under which he is to live is being claimed more widely and more insistently than ever before, it must seem most opportune that the work in which this doctrine is first clearly put before the peoples of modern Europe is to be given a form suited to its

importance.   Certainly American democracy, if it is to work
out the mission with which it seems to be entrusted, cannot
afford to refuse the support or to neglect the warnings it may
derive from a study of Marsiglio's ardent plea for a Peace of
the world based upon a just balance of social classes.